CHASING
EXTRAORDINARY

A 'HOW TO' GUIDE FOR NEWBIE
MARATHON RUNNERS

NICOLA LOVE

Let's Tell Your Story Publishing
London

COPYRIGHT

CONTENTS

'If you want to run, run a mile.
If you want to experience a different life,
run a marathon.'
~ Emil Zatopek

INTRODUCTION

ABOUT ME

Hey, Nikki here... howdy.

When I was a young girl I had big dreams of travelling the world. I wanted to see all the places.

I was also a runny, bouncy, jumpy thingy with lots of energy to burn.

That little girl has grown into a woman who still has a desire to run and bounce and jump and, with my love of running, I intend to discover all the places by foot. Pushing my physical boundaries by running, jogging, walking, staggering, crawling – and yes I've moved in all of these ways – I will simply do whatever it takes to achieve my goals.

Why do I push myself and then want to share the 'how to' tools I've gathered and the stories I've gained?

I have shelves full of books written by other runners and adventurers telling stories of their physical challenges. These books stoked a flame inside me to want to go and do something similar.

My hope is that I can do the same for someone who is like me – someone who has looked out into the world to find other people who have said – I can do that, other people who have dreamt big and then followed through and achieved.

I'm really a very average runner. I've placed in some races. I've middled in most. I've come last. Truthfully, I don't care about these things now. When I was younger I cared.

These days my love for adventure running, getting out in the world, seeing new places and challenging myself is what it's all about for me.

I'm ambitious, that's true. I'm ambitious to push my boundaries and see how far I can go.

How far is that?

I don't know. The best answer I can give is to say 'til the end'.

This gives me my drive, my purpose, my get up and go every day.

If I can help people along the way – encourage, support, inspire – then that is most definitely the icing on the cake.

So, here's my little guide that I'm throwing into the mix. If you want to run a marathon, stay less injured, seek adventures, and care for your body with running, here's my 'How To'.

And now it's over to you.

Think Big. Then Do.

I'd love for us to meet and run one day.

After all, anything is possible when you're Chasing Extraordinary!

WHO THIS BOOK IS FOR

You want to do it – that ultimate distance which runners aspire too.

It's a thought that's been running around inside your mind now for quite some time?

You want to run a marathon, but you wonder – Can you really?

So, I'm asking...

Can you imagine this?

> *You're covered in sweat. You've grimaced at times and yet your smile is as broad as your face.*
>
> *You hurt and yet you feel totally elated.*
>
> *You questioned if you really could, but you're about to make it.*
>
> *This race pushed you. You gave it everything you've got. You dedicated 6 months (and more) to making this big dream a reality.*
>
> *It challenged and tested your physical boundaries, but you've taken every single step of the 26.2 miles to go above and beyond them.*
>
> *You hear the crowd clapping and cheering as you head towards that finish line.*
>
> *You see the sea of smiling faces watching in awe of what you're about to do.*
>
> *And as you finally cross that 26.2 mile finish line you prove to yourself that you can do anything that you set your mind too.*

It's now time for you to make this dream a reality!

Not everyone will understand your need to fulfil this dream.

Are you crazy? Do you have a death wish? What are you running away from? Why?

These are questions that will be asked of you.

I know, because I've heard them all.

You'll question yourself – Why do I want to train today? It's too cold, it's too wet, it's snowing, it's too hot, it's too dark.

Your dedication will be questioned by others – Do you really need to run today? Come out with us and run on another day. Why do you need to run for that long? Blah, blah, blah.

Knowing your why will be key during these times.

Knowing your why will help you stay dedicated to making the time and energy available to train.

Knowing your why will keep you focussed and motivated.

Yes, I know that many people run marathons to raise money for charity or in dedication to important people in their lives.

However, ultimately it is you and only you who will do the months and months of training.

It will be you and only you who will take every single step of the 26.2 miles of a marathon.

It's crucial to understand WHY this is so important to you.

This book is for people who not only want to dream and imagine but want to experience that feeling of pride, of utter joy, of total self-belief that you can run a marathon.

MARATHON – HOW DO YOU DO THAT

I remember running my first half-marathon. It was during the Melbourne Marathon sometime in the '90s... I'm getting old I don't remember the exact year but I do remember doing it.

What I remember is finishing that race and watching the folk who continued on to complete the full marathon.

I was completely spent and I wondered how the hell you ever go twice that distance.

That was my first thoughts about marathon running, and that's when my inner running program began.

If you haven't got the inner game going on – the mind, the nutrition, the training, the resting and the mind (yep said it twice because it's so, so important), then you'll struggle to run long.

I've struggled on many occasions, despite having had some great coaching and being a fitness professional.

I've made lots of mistakes over the years, but an alternative way of looking at it is that I've had a lot of 'learning experiences'.

Hopefully, by reading this, you'll have a shorter learning curve than me.

WHAT THIS BOOK COVERS

This book provides all the tools you need to run a marathon including how to stay motivated, how to improve your technique, how to nourish your body and, of course, the training plans.

There's a week by week training plan that takes you from 10k to half-marathon to full marathon distance.

But hey, if you're starting as a complete newbie runner, I've totally got you covered. There's also a 0-5k-10k plan in there too.

It also provides a simple but effective understanding of how your body works, how it performs better, feels better, lasts longer when you look after it so that running becomes and stays a part of your life forever.

My aim for this book is to provide you with all the technical stuff, but hey I'm a real person who's gone through many ups and downs and sideways and tumbles.

That's why, in amongst the technical stuff, I've added a few of my own chasing extraordinary stories that have impacted my life for the better.

In terms of running marathons, my results are average.

However, what I lack in speed, I make up for with determination, dedication, education and life experiences.

I'm a body movement geek, who indulges her passion for running by running marathons and I believe anyone can run a marathon without facing these issues:

- overtraining
- falling out of love with running
- suffering excessive injuries
- always feeling totally knackered
- losing motivation
- feeling not ready

You just need a plan and some tools.

Let's take a look at the chapters in a little more detail.

CHAPTER 1: THE WHY

KNOW YOUR MOTIVATION, STAY FOCUSSED AND OVERCOME YOUR SELF-DOUBTS

Apparently, not everybody wants to run a marathon – who knew?... but I know you do and I want to help you stay totally connected to your goal.

Here are the benefits you get from running marathons.

A true understanding of dedication, devotion and commitment to yourself. You have to give these to yourself to train, to rest, to push your boundaries.

Self-love, self-appreciation, self-confidence. These are all super-powers you build by pushing your boundaries to run a marathon.

Self-love is definitely top of the agenda. You really have to care for yourself to be able to run that distance. You need to train, nourish, rest, believe and of course, dedicate yourself to your cause and your cause is you.

It saddens me when people say I'd love to run but 'things' get in the way. They either don't get going or they lose the motivation to keep going.

Issues like:

- lack of time
- work
- family life
- injuries
- age

are the most common roadblocks that come up, and may surface in your thoughts.

However, by working on your WHY, you'll have the mindset to stay true to your goal.

If you were to watch the London Marathon or any other marathon, and really look closely at the runners who challenge themselves to run 26.2 miles, then I'm pretty sure most in that crowd will have had to overcome one or several of these roadblocks.

If they can, then why not you?

Personally, there have been 3 times in my life when I've been unable to run. I've broken my leg twice and I've been pregnant once.

Without running I'm a bit of a pain in the ass to live with (so I've been told).

This is part of my WHY. I know it, I accept it and I 'run' with it.

CHAPTER 2: THE BASICS

THE 7 ESSENTIAL INGREDIENTS AND WHAT, HOW, WHEN AND WHY THEY HELP YOU TO RUN AND REDUCE OVERTRAINING AND INJURIES

By basics I mean, what you train, how you train and why these all come together so nicely and neatly to reduce the risk of overtraining and preventable injuries.

I say preventable simply because I have broken my leg. Twice. Both times accidentally, not through excessive training.

Just wanted you to know in case you'd seen me in a cast and thought 'hey that running lark can't be all that great, you've broken your leg... twice'.

Anyhoo...

What you train and why – I'll introduce you to the 7 essential ingredients:

- endurance
- speed
- strength
- power
- flexibility
- mobility
- agility

These are all the technical terms and sound a bit boring. In plain talk these things will help you run longer, stronger, with less stress and strain on your body – hope you agree, that sounds better.

How you train and why, using the 3-week block system. It's a system I was taught by my first running coach, Tony Benson, many moons ago.

Over the years and with added learning and life experiences (ie., having to juggle work, family and ageing), I've tweaked and changed the system to include my body movement geeky stuff.

However, the principal of training hard for 2 weeks then easing, testing and consolidating for one week remains the same.

The training plans combine all of these things and help me and the people I coach, to run marathons without overtraining, without falling out of love with running and staying as injury free as possible.

When you train and why – Ok, you want to run a marathon. Which means you'll need to train. Which means you'll need to know your lead time.

Which means you'll need to know where you're starting from, how much time you'll need to prepare for your race and how much time you'll need to commit each week.

You can enter a marathon then work out a training plan to fit into that timeframe.

Or you can work out the optimal lead time you'll need to train to achieve your marathon goal.

Either way works.

How you feel during the run and after the run may differ.

CHAPTER 3: THE TECHNIQUE

IMPROVE YOUR RUNNING PATTERN TO GET FASTER,
STRONGER AND REDUCE INJURIES

Most runners start by heading out the door and running until they stop or get back home again, whichever comes first.

They give little or no thought to optimum technique.

It's just go forward until you get puffed. Walk a bit. Then go again. Until you're done for the session.

I get it.

It's exactly the way I started.

Though I had a cheeky little head start.

I had done ballet from the age of four, and from that age, I was taught to pull my tummy in, squeeze my butt, stand tall, relax the upper body, look graceful and then move – POSTURE!

These 'posture' techniques were drummed into me pretty much on a daily basis for twelve years. They became a positive habit and a pretty solid base to start running from.

It's my turn now to drum them into you... they really are that important!

Ever heard anyone say running's bad for your knees, bad for your joints, bad for your back?

Well, it's true if you have poor technique and poor posture.

Many injuries occur due to weaknesses in the body and poor technique.

We'll discuss standing posture, running posture.

Then we'll get into the spicy added ingredients that help you look and feel better when you're running including:

- cadence
- foot landing
- arm swing

I love watching people change their running pattern and seeing how different they look. When I follow up later and ask how their running is progressing, I pretty much always hear how good their body feels.

That makes me happy.

CHAPTER 4: THE RECOVERY

SMARTEN UP YOUR RECOVERY PLAN AND FEEL GOOD

As I mentioned, running a marathon, or running any distance for that matter is all about self-love, and self-love is giving your body the TLC it needs.

You're asking it to do extraordinary things, and it will when it's cared for.

Like the training part, the recovery part is up to you. Take time, listen and feel your body. Your body will thank you for it.

We'll cover:

- stretching and tuning into your body
- foam rolling
- self-massage

Taking the time to do the pre-run care and the after-run care will help keep you feeling good, moving good and running good.

CHAPTER 5: THE NUTRITION

FUEL YOUR BODY TO RUN LONGER AND FEEL MORE
ENERGETIC

There's no way around it, your body needs food to function.

It's all about creating lifetime eating habits (no fad diets here) that fuel your body and give it the nourishment it needs to keep you running long and strong.

In this chapter I'll show you how simple it is to:

- build a plate at each meal that works for your body
- plate up meals with foods that tickle your tastebuds
- get all the proteins, fats and carbohydrates that you specifically need – we are all different

I've tried so many fad diets including the one where you simply don't eat – it was not a wise choice but I was young and silly.

Thankfully, it lead to a fascination to learn a more sustainable way of eating that cares for my body rather than breaks it – a way that gives me the energy I need and keeps me in a shape that I'm happy with.

What I've learned is how to balance life with some of my favourite things (cake and chocolate) using the 80/20 rule and my food mantra.

CHAPTER 6: THE PLAN

LAST BUT NOT LEAST, YOUR MARATHON TRAINING PLAN

To get to marathon distance you have to hit all the milestones along the way. There are no shortcuts (I've checked).

The key is to start.

And once you start, keep going.

You'll need to pass the 5k, the 10k and the half-marathon distances. So, I've provided training plans for all of them.

Running is going to be a part of your life for at least the next 6 months and my hope is that you'll fall so in love with running that you'll continue it on after you've run your first marathon.

Perhaps we'll even get the opportunity to run a marathon together?

All the training plans that you'll you need include:

- 0-5k–10k training plan
- 10k to half-marathon training plan
- half-marathon to full marathon training plan
- warm ups
- body workouts
- stretches

CHAPTER 7: THE DAY

WHAT HAPPENS ON RACE DAY AND LOTS OF OTHER FAQS ABOUT RUNNING AND TRAINING FOR A MARATHON

It's finally race day and you want to be fully prepared.

In this chapter, I give you all the hints and tips I've picked up along the way that will help your day run smoothly.

I also touch on other frequently asked questions that pop up during your training including:

- dealing with illnesses and injuries
- bucket list marathons (yep I'm that confident you'll want to do another)

HOW TO USE THIS BOOK

As you read through this book you'll be prompted to do some tasks:

- some writing regarding your WHY
- some technical tasks to help with your HOW
- oh, and of course, there's the practical week by week training plan of the WHAT to do

To make this easy for you, I've created PDFs that you can download and either type onto and print off, or print off and write on.

There are click links to the PDFs throughout the document for you to click through and print off as you go.

 Or, if you're like me and want to read everything first and then access the resources, all the PDFs are also listed again at the end of the book in the resources section. Look out for this icon.

Whilst the book is a do it yourself 'how to' guide that takes you from start to finish to become a marathon runner, I would still love to be a part of your marathon team.

As well as downloading all the PDFs in the Resources section there's a Let's get social section with all the magic links for us to meet up.

I'd love to say howdy, hear what you're up to and for you to meet up with other newbies, who soon become experienced marathon runners, just like you.

ON YOUR MARKS, GET SET, GO!

So, now you know where we're heading, let's get your marathon on!

'At mile 20 I thought I was dead
At mile 22 I wished I was dead
At mile 24 I knew I was dead
At mile 26.2 I realised I'd become too tough to kill'
~ Anon

CHAPTER 1. THE WHY

YOUR MOTIVATION TO SUCCEED

'Create the day that creates your success'
~ Nikki Love

What are your motivations?

What does success look like to you?

Knowing the answer to these 2 important questions will help you stay true to your training plans and help you achieve your marathon dream goal.

I may be making a big assumption here, but you're reading this 'How to' guide because I'm guessing that running a marathon is a dream goal.

Let's take a good look at this.

What will success 'training, running and completing a marathon' look like to you?

I'm going to get you to do a little exercise.

Not the sweaty, heavy-breathing type – though I do want you to get excited and whip yourself into an emotional frenzy.

If you truly have no experience or no idea, then I definitely recommend getting yourself down to a marathon finish line to take in the whole experience.

If you're like me, you'll love every minute of it and maybe shed a little emotional tear (tears of awe and joy by the way).

It'll also be like having ants in your pants – you'll want to be a part of it, you'll want it to be you crossing that finish line with the sweat and glowing smile of someone who did.

It's a great experience to get your motivational juices flowing.

Anyway, back to the exercise.

WHAT YOUR 'SUCCESS' LOOKS LIKE

Pen and paper ready... picture yourself at the end of your marathon. Visualise it and now write about it with all the emotion you can muster.

My success story

1. How do I feel at the end?

   Describe your pride, joy, feeling of absolute self-belief.

2. Why do I want to run a marathon?

   List all the reasons/motivations for wanting to run a marathon and be truly honest – do you want to lose weight, feel mentally strong, earn bragging rights, show doubters that you can do it.

3. What has it meant to me to cross the finish line?

   Describe how you've trained, you've dedicated, you've committed a lot of time and energy to achieving this goal.

4. What does the finish line look like?

   Describe the atmosphere, the noise, the smells, the sights; be as descriptive as you can.

5. What does my success look like?

   Describe what you are achieving out of this life experience.

Download

I have attached a printable PDF version of these questions in the resources section at the end of the book, so you can put a lot of thought into this exercise and, most importantly, read it regularly.

This is my secret sauce that has helped me achieve the things that I have. I really recommend that you do it too.

I've gone through this exercise many times and I'm really clear on my WHY motivations and what success looks like to me.

Let me share...

Release the crazy

Without running I'm a nightmare!

If I can't be a runny, jumpy, bouncy thing I get stir crazy, grumpy and a pain in the ass to live with. This is part of my motivation to keep running.

I also realised in my early teens that running was a great way to counter my vices. I love chocolate. I love cake.

Hey, whilst I'm fessing up I also love wine and beer (though I promise you, mum and dad, that the wine and beer came about in my teens, my much later teens).

Yep, I'm a chocolate eating, cake scoffing, wine slugging, beer drinking fitness professional that runs and trains her little butt off to offset her... wilder side.

But shouldn't I be like 'my body is a temple' and all that jazz?

Well yep, most of the time I am... but some of the time I'm not.

However, all of the time I want my body to look good and feel good so I train and eat to achieve that.

Next motivation.

Buzz and adventure

Running gives me a buzz – a happy buzz.

It's all to do with these happy chemicals that are released into the body during exercise – dopamine, serotonin and endorphins.

If you want to read more, I recommend the book 'Change Your Brain Change Your Body' by Dr Daniel G Amen.

In short...

Dopamine is the chemical of motivation, it helps you overcome low motivation and low energy. You can boost your dopamine levels by doing intense physical exercise. Running ticks that box.

Serotonin is the chemical of feeling peaceful and happy. It helps you overcome anxiety and depression. You can boost your serotonin levels by doing physical activity. Another tick for running.

Endorphins are chemicals linked to feeling pleasure and eliminating pain. You can boost endorphin release through exercise, which is where you hear the term 'runner's high'.

If you're a runner, you'll know what I'm on about.

If you're not a runner but you're thinking of becoming a runner, these are the 'feel goods' to seek.

There's also the chemical adrenalin and I'll admit I'm a bit of an adrenalin junkie.

When I run in places I don't know and I'm a little frightened of my surroundings (yeah, that happens) or I'm lining up to do a run that seems beyond me, that experience gives me an adrenalin high.

And lastly...

Life choice

My why is because I choose a 'life' wish.

If I don't chase my big goals, if I don't live my big dreams, if my ambitions go unfulfilled, then the dreamer, the ambitious, the tenacious, the super-strong- willed Nikki inside of me will die.

I don't want to look back and say 'I wish I had'.

I intend to look back and say 'wow, look what I did!'

Success to me is:

> *Being my best. Having fun. Being adventurous. Keeping on running into my 50s and 60s and beyond. Running around the world seeing as much of it as I can. Inspiring, encouraging, supporting and helping others who have an urge inside them to push their boundaries and chase their extraordinary.*

As well as spending time determining what my success looks like for the big picture, I also do a daily practice of journaling, visualising, manifesting, dreaming big, call it what you will.

I write.

I write every day about having completed the event I'm training for.

And somewhere in my brain, it believes that it has already occurred, because my brain has thought it and seen it and believes it to be real.

It's a weird ol' thing the brain...

Even when your body hasn't had first-hand experience, if you visualise and write about it then your my mind believes it.

If you want to read more on this topic then I definitely recommend 'The Power of Neuro-plasticity' by Shad Helmstetter, Ph.D.

> *You can take charge of your mind's programming – who you are, how you feel, what you think, what your attitude is, what actions you take, and what you choose to do next. But you have to wire your brain with what you want it to do next...*
>
> *Neural activity feedback loop – You think in a self-directed way (the success result you imagine). Your brain 'gets it' and records your thoughts. When you repeat the same thoughts often enough, your brain wires them into neural pathways and connects them to other similar pathways you've already stored. Your brain then sends those same messages back to you as 'thoughts', 'beliefs' and 'attitudes' that you act on.*

If you haven't got the time to read the book, then follow these simple principles about visualising/journaling.

Write about the event that you are training for as if you have already achieved it. For example:

> *'I am a marathon runner. I am a London marathon finisher. Finishing the London marathon was the most exciting, thrilling experience I've ever had...'*

Now keep writing as if you've already completed it.

I do this daily.

I also have 'My Success Story' that I've poured my heart into next to my bed so that I can look at it and read it regularly.

Write to your mind, it will believe you and it will help you to make the choices you need to take along the way.

This is how you stay motivated!

Yes, you will run when it's cold, wet and miserable. Yes, you will run when people question your sanity, question your dedication, offer you alternatives.

Why?

Because connecting with your how, what and why you want to feel will keep you going.

Truly wanting to experience achieving your goals will keep you going and keep you working with purpose towards the success you truly believe you can achieve.

Dream big. Write daily. Then do!

SELF-DOUBT

*'Whatever the mind of man can conceive and believe,
it can achieve'
~ Napoleon Hill*

I believe that anyone can run a marathon. Why? The 2016 London Marathon celebrated its one millionth runner to pound the pavements from Black Heath to St James Park. True there will have to be some repeat customers in that total – I've done it 3 times.

But honestly, if you were to take a good look at those million people and truly look at the variations:

- age
- gender
- shape
- size
- fitness
- health

I'm pretty sure there'd be someone in that crowd that you could relate too.

Now I'm going to stick my neck out and say none of these things should be a roadblock to you running a marathon.

You just gotta wanna do it!

Everyone in that crowd, from the winner to the elites, to the middle of the pack, right back to very last person who crossed that finish line... are just like you.

They all started as newbie marathoners.

They all gradually built up their distance and speed and they all took every single step to cover the 26.2 miles.

There are no short cuts.

There are no fast forward buttons from mile ten to mile twenty – although I've experienced not registering those miles passing by having been so totally lost in my thoughts. However, my feet, my body and my GPS were testament that I did actually travel them.

Let's debunk these 'issues'.

AGE

> *'Age is no barrier, it's a limitation you put on your mind'*
> *~ Jackie Joyner-Kersey*

Age is not a barrier.

Many of my clients took up running in their late 30s or early 40s and once they started, they realised it was something they really rather loved.

I also have a few who discovered that they were really rather good at it and have qualified as 'good for age' in races such as the London Marathon and the Chicago Marathon. Pretty amazing stuff!

That's not my story.

I'm a very average runner. I've realised that what I lack in speed, I make up for in tenacity – the will to keep going.

I only took up running with gusto in my early 30s, shortly after breaking my leg (the first time). Prior to that, it was a secondary activity to ballet and aerobics.

Remember the 1980s? It was all about the 'thong leotard' and I had a drawer full of them. I used running to keep my weight down and my butt thong-sized.

After I broke my leg I joined a triathlon club to rehab in the water and get my fitness back with the run/cycle shizzle. I loved triathlons but mainly I loved the running part of a triathlon and I really fell in love with the idea of going long. I started training for the ultimate – an Ironman triathlon.

Mid-ironman training, I moved to England, left my tri-bike with my folks in Australia and parked my thoughts of triathlon.

In the cold and grey of my first English winter, I concentrated on running.

Running was my 'me' time. Time to ease my mind and get to know my new home.

I spent a lot of time running along the paths of Nottingham's River Trent. It helped with my anxiety about living in a new place, being so far away from my family and friends and it fuelled the little adventurer inside me.

Anyhow back to the age thing. I entered my first marathon aged 34 and failed. I'd given birth to my kiddo 6 months prior and had done no training throughout the pregnancy and minimal in the following 6 months.

The following year I attempted and completed my second marathon with the biggest smile on my face.

Fast forward to my early 40s and, in the midst of a struggling business, a strained relationship and a low point of self-esteem, I set off to do 7 marathons in 7 days.

As I mentioned earlier, running marathons strengthens my inner belief and my self-confidence that I can do whatever I set my mind to.

At that time, I was in desperate need of these things.

I've just hit 50 and whilst many 50-year-olds around me are starting to slow it down, I've decided to crank it up and go the other way.

What a revelation this has been!

Once I started looking for role models in the lifestyle I was choosing, I discovered that at this age I'm only a spring chicken and that running marathons, running ultras, running extreme can be done in your 50s, 60s, 70s. Inspiring!

A man whose story has touched me immensely is Wally Hesseltine. At age 72 he attempted to become the eldest competitor to complete the Western States 100, a mountain run in which you have 30 hours to complete nearly four marathons.

Wally's attempt was made into a short video. It shows his progress throughout the 30 hours, it shares his story of how he got into running marathons and how running is an essential part of his life.

As the clock gets closer to timing out. Wally is starting to stagger. His running friends and supporters use their bodies to keep Wally upright and moving towards the finish line. He staggers, he drops to the ground, everyone is yelling words of support for Wally to get up.

Honestly, my words here will not justifiably describe how Wally crosses that finish line.

I simply recommend that you watch his video: https://vimeo.com/181118448.

Be prepared to be inspired, but have a box of tissues handy.

If you think you're too old, think again. At 72, Wally Hesseltine is a wonderful role model.

Another inspiration to me, and who's book 'A Little Run Around the World' put the seed into my head that I too can run around the world, is Rosie Swale Pope MBE.

The book was written by Rosie after she completed a 5-year self-supported circumnavigation of the world.

At aged 55!

She is now 70 years old and still a marathon runner. In fact, she just finished running across America. She is truly amazing!

Age is simply a number. If you want to run... run!

GENDER

'Baby we were born to run'
~ Bruce Springsteen

Okay, Bruce's song may not specifically be about running a marathon, but the majority of us are born with the body parts that enable us to learn to crawl, then to walk and then run about.

The ability to run has nothing to do with what bits you do or don't have tucked away in your underwear.

Prior to the early 1970s women were not allowed to enter marathon distance races. It was deemed too difficult an event for women.

In the 1967 Boston Marathon, a lady by the name of Kathryn Switzer was credited as the first woman to run a marathon race. Although the rules stated women could not enter, Switzer registered herself by using her initials and surname and by not declaring her gender.

There were actually 2 women in the race that day. The first female finisher, Bobbi Gibb ran unregistered.

A race official attempted to physically remove Switzer from the race. Thankfully for all future marathon women, she held her ground.

It took a further 5 years from that race before women were officially welcome to participate in a marathon. The race official who attempted to remove Switzer from the race was instrumental in the change of this rule – good man!

What is now being noticed is that on longer runs such as marathons and ultra's there is actually less discrepancy between the abilities of women and men.

In fact, women may have a hidden advantage over men when it comes to running long distances. It's to do with our levels of body fat.

Whether we like it or not ladies, we generally tend to hold a bit more body fat than men. However, this may actually help us over the long distance.

In simple term, our first port of call for energy when we do exerting exercise is our glycogen stores – this is the carbohydrates we consume and store in our body's cells.

We all store approximately 2 hours' worth of hard exertion in our cells, and as our body runs out of glycogen, we either have to top it up by refuelling, or our body will look to its other energy sources – fats and proteins.

It's suggested that women may be naturally more efficient at utilising their body fat stores earlier in a long distance race than men.

Just a side note – before you go thinking hey, all I have to do is run longer than 2 hours and I'll get rid of some excess body fat. Your body doesn't really work as simply as that.

Now, here's the funny ol' thing about the body.

If it thinks it's going into starvation mode ie., it's glycogen stores are being depleted and no food source is coming back in, then it will start holding on to its fat reserves for dear life and will start tapping into the source that is using up a lot of energy, but can also provide energy.

It starts tapping into its protein stores.

This is what we all want to avoid! Our protein stores are our muscles and when we start using this source, we are literally eating away at the things that are moving our body.

Not good for either gender!

Another hidden advantage women may have over men is our oestrogen levels.

No matter what gender, we all experience tired muscles during a marathon, however oestrogen (the primary female sex hormone) attaches to a neurotransmitter in the brain delaying a message saying that the body is getting fatigued.

Tricky little hormone.

So, take it as gospel from Bruce 'The Boss' Springsteen... *'Baby we were born to run'*.

SHAPE, SIZE, FITNESS AND HEALTH

'Whether you ran a mile in 4 minutes or 40 minutes,
you still ran a mile'
~ Anon

As I pounded the streets of London during my third London Marathon, which was also my 7th marathon in 7 days, I saw some very interesting sights.

I passed a woman who had a sign on her back which read...

'I've had 2 hip replacements. I'm 70 (something'ish)* and I'm still running.'

* I can't quite remember her age, but her sign struck a chord with me. If she can do it, so can I!

I passed 2 women who stopped just past the halfway point for a sneaky fag. I'm not a smoker, I don't understand the appeal and quite truthfully it confused my brain to watch them. However, I thought surely if they can do it, so can I!

I fought an awesome battle with a guy who was wearing a rhinoceros outfit.

At the time I was in awe of how anyone could carry anything other than themselves over such a long distance. Since running through the Amazon carrying a 10kg backpack on my own back, I truly understand what that dude had been going through.

Again, I thought if he can do it, so can I!

Lastly, I ran up alongside Mr Poopy Pants... but I'll expand on this story a little later.

My hero from afar, and one of the people who I drew inspiration from to do something extraordinary and run my 7 marathons is Sir Ranulph Fiennes.

In 2003, Sir Ranulph Fiennes undertook the extraordinary adventure of running 7 marathons in 7 days on 7 continents. Not only was this an extraordinary feat, he was 59 years old, and he completed it a mere four months after experiencing a heart attack and undergoing double heart by-pass surgery.

Honestly... wow! I mean... WOW!

I had the privilege of meeting Sir Ranulph Fiennes at the launch of his book 'Fear: Our Ultimate Challenge'.

I mentioned that his 7x7x7 challenge was an inspiration for me to undertake my challenge. He politely responded with 'You're welcome'. He also mentioned that he was glad there are only 7 and not 8 continents.

Now if there had been 8, I'm pretty certain Sir Ranulph would have been up to the task, but it's good to know that even the BEST of the BEST has fears and questions themselves.

WHEN NOT TO RUN

Having debunked all of the potential excuses above, it's still important to remember that running is exertion and if you've been advised not to run by your doctor, take heed.

Having a medical check-up before you take on any form of new exercise is always a wise move.

Honestly.

Go get a check-up before you start training.

AT A GLANCE

Running a marathon is going to take a lot of dedication, the key to staying motivated is to know your WHY.

Ask yourself the question 'What does success look like to you?'

Now write!

Be as graphic and as vivid and as totally engrossed as you can.

Describe how you will look and feel, what you will smell, hear and see, and write as if you have already completed the event.

1. **How do you feel at the end?**
   Your pride, joy, feeling of absolute self-belief
2. **Why did you want to run a marathon?**
   List all the reasons and be truly honest.
3. **What has it meant to you to cross that finish line?**
   You've trained, you've dedicated, you've committed a lot of energy to achieving this.
4. **What does the finish line look like?**
   The atmosphere, the noise, the smells, the sights, be as descriptive as you can...
5. **What does your success look like to you?**

Answer these questions and keep your document handy. Read, re-read and re-read as you train for your marathon.

Write every day. Tell your brain that it is already the person that it's training to be – a marathon runner.

With your 'WHY' firmly in place and your goal achievement written daily, there will be no room in your brain for any excuse to impact your dream.

WHAT'S NEXT

Now that we know anyone can run. Let's get into the things that will help you run.

'I've learned that finishing a marathon isn't just an athletic achievement. It's a state of mind; a state of mind that says anything is possible.'
~ John Hanc

CHAPTER 2. THE BASICS

THE 7 ESSENTIAL INGREDIENTS AND WHAT, HOW, WHEN AND
WHY THEY HELP YOU TO RUN AND REDUCE OVERTRAINING
AND INJURIES

Running is easy, you simply strap yourself into a pair of trainers,
step outside and move one foot in front of the other in a runny
styley type motion.

Yep, true.

But as a body movement geek, I see people... because they run.

They don't do any other beneficial stuff that helps them run with
fewer injuries along the way.

If you want to run a marathon, at some point you're gonna have
to run long and you're gonna have to run fast.

You're gonna need strength and power, and if you're like me and
love to do it on trails, then you'll definitely require some mobility,
agility and flexibility – though road running often requires these
skills too.

And this is where I see a lot of people fall apart.

Quite literally, they fall apart and come to see me for much
needed, but often avoidable, fixing therapy sessions.

Great for business.

But honestly, I don't want to see you injured, I want to keep you
out on the road.

So, here are the 7 essential ingredients that make up a well-
rounded training plan.

WHAT YOU TRAIN AND WHY

These 7 essential ingredients are all as important as each other to help keep you running long and as injury free as possible:

- endurance
- speed
- power
- strength
- mobility
- agility
- flexibility

ENDURANCE

To run a marathon you have to have it in you to keep on going.

There are 2 ways to 'have it in you'.

There's the knowing your 'Why' which we spoke about earlier.

Then there's the physical.

You need to physically build up your distance gradually.

By gradually I mean upping the distance of your last long run by 10-15% each week.

Using a 3-week cycle, you up the distance in week 1 and week 1, then consolidate in week 3. I expand more on 3-week cycles in 'How you train and why' a little further down.

Rinse and repeat.

There is a reason why I suggest only upping the distance by 10-15% regularly.

There's a slight lag in the time it takes for your body to get used to the exercise you put it through.

Aerobically you improve quickly. Your heart and lungs are the smart-ass kids on the block of your body.

They 'get it' quickly and only take a couple of weeks to get used to the physical exertion you're asking them to do.

This is when I see the injuries start showing up.

Your heart and lungs feel good, you feel aerobically fitter, so you push further. Unfortunately, it's often before the rest of your body has caught up with the process.

Physically, your muscles, ligaments, tendons and bones take a little longer to 'get it'. They lag behind in the process by a few weeks – dumbasses!

The slow increase and consolidation process tends to work better if it's longevity and injury prevention running that you're after.

For me, the idea of running as injury free for the rest of my life is really rather appealing, so I'm happy to go the slow and steady build and consolidate route.

SPEED

Why do you need speed when you're doing long?

I understand that for most, simply running at a steady pace to get from the start to the finish is all you want to do. Your training plan probably reflects that. You run 3-5 times a week, pretty much running at the same pace each session.

As much as I love running and I love the adventure of running for hours on end out in nature, I'm also a busy working mum and I don't have hours mid-week to spend lolloping about the countryside running at the same pace trying to improve my marathon.

Incorporating speed – short, sharp and intense – improves your fitness. Trust me, those long runs become so much easier when you've done hard and fast during the week.

Technically it's called working at your lactic threshold and marks the point at which your body is stopping working aerobically (with air) and you hit the anaerobic zone (without air).

We breathe air to live. You can't stay in the 'without air' zone for very long.

How do you know when you're training at lactic threshold?

Well, have you ever experienced that feeling when you're pushing so hard that you can feel your heart pounding almost out of your chest, your lungs are struggling to bring in air and your legs feel like they are on fire.

The chemical reactions occurring in your body when you work anaerobically (without air) will take you to a point where you can't go on anymore. That's hitting and going beyond your lactic threshold.

The aim with marathon speed work is to train your body to work at a higher heart rate without going over the lactic threshold tipping point.

Running at varying speeds (5k pace and 10k pace) and with varying recovery times to bring the heart rate back down in between the fast efforts, will help push up the ceiling of your lactic threshold.

By training just below your lactic threshold your heart becomes more efficient at pumping blood that carries around the oxygen that your body needs to keep it running at pace.

Now I understand that many will say – meh, I'm not that bothered about the time I do, I just want to run the marathon distance.

And for the most part, I'm with you.

However, there will be times that having speed in your body (the ability to kick) will come in handy.

Here's the story of Mr Poopy Pants to inspire you to do speed work.

As I was coming to the final stretch of the 2010 London Marathon, which I pointed out earlier was my 7th marathon in 7 days, I ran up alongside a bloke who had, quite literally, pooped his pants.

Unfortunately, he was wearing light lycra pants and his 'problem' was on show for all to see.

Now I have to commend the dude for keeping on keeping on when he was obviously having a bad day.

But c'mon.

I had just run 183 miles in 7 days. I was about to turn the bend and run towards the finish line – with all of the crowds and all of the cameras.

Yes, I was being vain, but there was no bloody way I was going to cross that finish line running next to Mr Poopy Pants.

I found something inside of me. My body remembered the speed work I had put it through.

And I kicked.

I left that guy far behind me and crossed the finish line without Mr Poopy Pants spoiling my photo.

I also had a rather terrifying experience of being hissed and growled at on the last bit of my epic 5-day Jungle Ultra race.

> *My headtorch was shining into the jungle and something in that jungle did not take a shine to my shine. Honestly, I nearly became Ms Poopy Pants.*
>
> *Two thoughts entered my head 'Oh shit, jaguar' and 'Gotta get home to my boy'.*
>
> *With my heart literally pounding out of my chest, I turned my head so that the light was no longer shining in that direction. I moved quietly and quickly away occasionally checking back behind me and then ran as fast and as far as my tired legs could take me.*
>
> *It wasn't far. I was pretty cooked by that stage of the event. Thankfully no big hissy-growly cat thingy chased me down.*

Speed work. Get it done or run alongside Mr Poopy Pants or get bitten on the bum by a jaguar. Your choice!

POWER

Power is all about explosive energy and there are 2 ways to train your power.

Hills baby!

I know, hills are often the nemesis of most runners. However, get good at them and the flats feel like a doddle.

Yes, hill sessions are similar to speed sessions in that you'll find yourself working near your lactic threshold. However, it's more about working the springiness in your legs to improve explosive power.

Hill sessions are about keeping good posture and using your body and core strength to keep you upright whilst driving the knee upwards to spring forward.

Now I have gone up many hills where springing was simply not possible (well not for me).

I've had to scramble and crawl and haul my butt up some unbelievably steep inclines.

However, having 'power' training in my core and legs helped explode my back leg up and drive my knee forward to inch my way up the tough terrain.

It's an important tool to have in your toolkit.

The other training that improves power is the bouncy, springy, jumpy stuff in the bodyweight workouts. These type of exercises are otherwise known as plyometrics.

As I mentioned, I'm a body movement geek and my goal is to keep your body balanced and as injury free as possible.

Due to the nature of us being humans, we tend to be one-side more dominant – right handed, left handed.

This one-side dominance often reflects when we do exercises that use both sides at the same time (such as squats) – the dominant side tends to take over and do more of the work without you consciously noticing it.

Additionally, due to the nature of running, we tend to only move in one direction – forward.

So, the exercises that I recommend for you on your non-running days are designed to improve your power and keep your body balanced – working the right side and left side by themselves – and moving it in other directions.

This helps avoid injury and in turn, keeps you on the training track rather than on the injury bench.

How do you know if you're imbalanced or one side is more dominant than the other?

Well, I'll take you through some body movement assessment exercises at the end of this chapter which will show you areas that may need some work.

STRENGTH

Lack of body strength is another common reason why people come and see me with injuries when they go long.

When you go long, you get tired. When you get tired and you lack body strength, you lose posture. When you lose posture, you put pressure on your joints and bones – you get injured!

Becoming a bodybuilder is not the place I want to take you to, but having body strength is super important for going long and running marathons.

I'm talking about strength in your core, along your spine, across your chest and back, in your arms as well as those things way, way down there... your legs.

I meet so many people – guys, gals, young, old and everything in between who, when I ask, say they don't do anything other than run. Despite being a fitness professional, I've occasionally fallen into this trap, much to my body's detriment. Learn from my mistakes.

Body strength is now one of the key components included in my training plan and should be a part of yours. It will be a part of yours if you chose to follow the plans in this book.

I don't want you spending a lot of your precious time doing exercises that are okay for general fitness or are in the bodybuilding realm.

Instead, I hone in on the exercises that give you the most bang for your buck and are the most beneficial to your running. Remember, we don't want marathon training to completely take over your life or for you to feel overwhelmed by the amount of training required. We want it to be a welcome addition to your lifestyle.

That's why I provide exercises that enhance your running by improving your core strength, strengthen your postural muscles, improve power and keep your body balanced... targeted, practical and efficient. Good for running. Good for life.

Exercises such as single-leg push ups are terrific for runners. They strengthen the upper body as well as engaging the core and back muscles to keep the body stable through the movement.

Adding movement to an exercise such as doing a burpee, is one of my favourite non-running exercises for runners.

The addition of movement – specifically jumping the legs out to the rear to get into the push up position without dipping in the lower back and then whipping the legs back underneath the body using the core muscles really works the strength and coordination of all the body.

Single leg push up   **Burpee push up**

I'll also get you to do a lot of single-legged exercises. This helps to keep the body balanced in terms of equal power and strength in each leg as well as working on your balance ie., not falling over.

Exercises such as single-leg squats, single-leg deadlifts, single-leg tuck jumps and skater jumps will quickly show you if there are any discrepancies between your right and left sides.

When you do these exercises, look and feel for differences be-tween the right and left. Things you may notice include:

- Squat depths – Can you go deeper? Do you struggle on the up?
- Jump heights – Have you got more power? Do you have more control?
- Balance – Are you more stable or do you wobble about? Do your knees cave right across the mid-line of your body or do they point way out to the side?

*Your knee and toes should be pointing forward and be directly underneath your hip during these exercises – before you move, and when you land.

Single leg squat

Single leg deadlift

It's quite common to find differences. It's why I get you to work on it.

Often it's simply a matter of technique practice. You may not be used to doing exercises such as these, so it may be a learning curve.

If there is a difference, then hopefully by doing these exercises regularly you'll notice changes and improvements to your weaker side.

If you experience pain during any of these exercises then I recommend getting yourself checked over by a professional – osteopath, physiotherapist, chiropractor, sports therapist.

If after 4-6 weeks there is still a very marked discrepancy, I'd also recommend seeing a professional therapist.

The reason I'm so keen for you to build a stronger and balanced body is that any weaknesses are consolidated in our daily patterns.

If you are running long distance then you are holding that pattern for a very long time.

You may simply need a little tweak of your body or more specific rehabilitation exercises to address your specific weakness.

You'll find full details of the Workouts in Chapter 6 – The Plan.

MOBILITY, AGILITY AND FLEXIBILITY

Although I've lumped these 3 together, they are different but they work cohesively together.

When I talk about mobility I'm talking about the joints.

Maintaining good joint mobility comes from having good posture, keeping the body balanced and keeping the muscles supple.

Agility is the ability to move quickly from one position to another. This requires good suppleness of the muscles and mobility of the joints to allow changes of direction. Agility is the ability to go over, under and through obstacles (which you get a lot of when you run trails).

It comes in handy for road races too. Being able to move quickly to avoid crashing into other runners when they change direction or decide to stop in front of you is useful. It happens a lot. As does having to avoid landing on discarded water bottles and cups at race drink stations as you pass through them.

These are the 7 basic ingredients that make up a marathon training plan that gets you running long and keeps you injury free.

HOW YOU TRAIN AND WHY

I use the 3-week system. Train hard for 2 weeks then ease off and consolidate for the third week. Rinse and repeat.

The 2 weeks of hard training are just that. You run, work on your body strength, push yourself.

In week 3 you ease off. You rest your body before testing it to record your improvement in speed and stamina.

This rest, test and consolidate week is really important.

It's the week that gives you a break mentally and physically. Remember I want you to stay in love with running. Rest and seeing results helps with this process.

And you will see results. Your time trials in week 3 will improve if you do the work. These time trials set your predicted marathon time and your pace goals for your long training runs.

When you run at your predicted marathon pace you build up the mental strength that tells you "YES!" you will be ready on marathon day.

This 3-week system is the same for a newbie marathoner right through to a 'good for age' athlete.

The training plan is all about creating long-term training habits right from the get go.

For example, let's take a look at one of the hill sessions.

> ### Hill B training session
>
> *Find a hard gradient hill more than 60 seconds to sprint up*
>
> *30-60 minutes including 10 x (30secs @ L9 up / 1:30secs recovery down). Mark your start place and sprint up for 30 secs, mark that spot and recover down to start position. The aim is to continue to hit initial sprint distance up for each repeat in the session and improve the distance of the spot each week. Recover back to the start position either using all the time or resting at the bottom, but use the full 1:30 for recovery. Record the distance.*

Find a hill, a good steep hill. A hill that will take longer than 30 seconds to run up it at fast pace.

The reason?

As your strength, power and endurance improve, you will cover more ground in the 30 seconds.

As a newbie runner, you will push to your own ability during the 30 seconds up.

You may get 50 metres up the hill.

It will probably then take you all of the 1 minute 30 seconds to walk recover back down to your starting place – so you'll get little or no rest time at the bottom before you have to power up again.

The length of training time during this session is a little less at the start of the plan, but it builds as you get stronger.

As you get stronger the distance that you can achieve during the 30 seconds up (the 50 metres or such) will increase.

The time it takes for you to get back to your start position during the 1:30min recovery will decrease and you'll get more rest at the bottom.

You will see progress. You will see your speed, strength and endurance build as you create long-term training habits.

Now I mentioned body strength training. These sessions are a great opportunity to work on any particular weaknesses you may have and, as it says on the tin, build body strength.

How do you know if you have weaknesses?

Let's take a look at some simple body movement exercises and take note of how and what moves and if there is any pain, tightness, or weakness.

DIY BODY MOVEMENT ASSESSMENT

Here are a few simple exercises that challenge your body and will highlight areas that may be weaker and can be improved upon on your non-run days.

The aim of the training plan is to improve your running as well as strengthening your body.

I'd recommend that you come back to these exercises every 3 weeks during the consolidation week and give yourself a body check-up.

 I have attached a printable PDF version of these tests in the Resources section at the end of the book, so you can keep a record of how your body is feeling and the improvements you are making.

Download

I have also included a video demonstration of the test movements, the links are in the book and the PDF.

FRONT PLANK

 https://youtu.be/TZ2H1MAIVUs

The aim of this exercise is to test your core and back strength.

1. Lay on your belly then come up onto your elbows,making sure they are directly below your armpit. Keep your hands apart and your eyes looking at the ground slightly out in front of you.
2. Come up onto the balls of your feet and get your butt, shoulders and head in a horizontal line and hold that position.
3. Time yourself – aiming for a maximum of 90 seconds.

When you are in the position notice if you are struggling to hold the straight line? Is your lower back dipping? Are you wobbling as the time ticks on?

Score yourself using this table.

Time	Score
Experience Pain	0
Leaning of body left/right Body raised < 45°	1
Body raised between 45° and upright	2
Body fully raised Head in line with hands	3

STRAIGHT LEG RAISE

 https://youtu.be/6uU9iC1UiDA

This exercise tests the flexibility of your hamstrings. You may also notice tightness in your calves.

1. Find the protruding part of your hip bone and knee cap and mark on your thigh the halfway point between both.
2. Lay down on your back and place a marker on the ground in line with the mark you made on your thigh.
3. Pull your toes up and towards your body.
4. Keeping the leg straight, raise one leg up as high as you can. Repeat to the other side.

As you move into this position, feel and take note of how and where your body is feeling any tightness or stiffness.

Score yourself using this table.

Time	Score
Experience Pain	0
Knee does not reach your halfway marker	1
The knee but not ankle pass halfway marker	2
Knee and ankle pass halfway marker	3

SINGLE LEG LUNGE (RIGHT AND LEFT)

 https://youtu.be/poJkjalJlOI

The aim of this exercise is to test the strength and stability of your quads and ankles. If you are doing this on your own, do it in front of a mirror. If you have someone to help, get them to watch your knees, ankles and upper body as you move.

1. Mark a straight line on the ground (use a mat, or mark a line) and grab a pole, stick, broom – you are going to hold this behind your back.
2. Put your feet along the line, right foot out in front, left behind and practice a lunge so that your left knee touches the heel of your right foot – your feet are now the right distance apart.
3. Grab hold of your stick behind your back, your right hand holding on above your head, your left hand holding on at your waist.
4. Lower yourself slowly into the lunge aiming to keep your front knee in line with your toes, then rise back up again.
5. Repeat to the other side – both feet on the line, left foot forward, create the space for the lunge so the right knee touches the heel of the left foot. Hold the stick, left arm above the head, right hand at the waist and move into the lunge.

As you move into this position, feel and take note of how and where your body moves. Do you wobble about? Does your upper body lean to one side? Does your knee drop across the centre line instead of staying in line with your toes.

Score yourself using this table.

Time	Score
Experience Pain	0
Loss of balance. Big movement of spine forwards or sideways	1
Alignment is lost between knee and foot	2
Knee and feet in line, no movement of spine	3

PUSH UP HALF, FULL

 https://youtu.be/hz13hiT5lxQ

The aim of this exercise is to test your core, back and upper body strength.

Half push up:

1. Start on your knees, take your arms out in front so that your body weight is over your arms and make sure your hands are directly beneath your arms pits, eyes looking out slightly in front of your hands.
2. Keep your tummy tucked in and your back straight as you lower your body down towards the floor leading with the chest and aiming for your nose to hit the ground.
3. Keep your tummy tight and the back straight (don't let the lower back move or dip), as you bring the body back up to the starting position.

Full push up

1. Start on the balls of your feet, your arms extended and make sure your hands are directly beneath your arms pits, eyes looking out slightly in front of your hands.
2. Keep your tummy tucked in and your back straight, as you lower your body down towards the floor leading with the chest and aiming for your nose to hit the ground.
3. Keeping the tummy tight and the back straight (don't let the lower back move or dip), bring the body back up to the starting position.

As you move into this position, feel and take note of how or where your body moves. Do you wobble about? Can you get down, but not get back up again? Does your lower back dip to get back up?

I'm not going to get you to score this exercise, but I do want you to take note of how strong the movement feels. You'll be doing a lot of push ups in the body strength workouts and the more you do the stronger your whole body becomes.

The stronger your whole body becomes then the better you will hold your body throughout your marathon run.

My aim is for you to be able to do full push ups as well as run a marathon by the end of your training.

I'm a pushy little coach, but I've always got your best intentions at heart.

WHEN TO TRAIN AND WHY

Okay, you've got this thing inside your head – you want to run a marathon.

Do you enter one first and then work out a training plan in the timeframe you have, or do you work out how much time you'll need to train from your current starting place to achieve your ultimate marathon goal and then look at marathons around that projected date?

Either way works.

How you feel during the run and after the run may differ.

If you are a newbie at marathon training and you enter a marathon for 3 months' time – sure you could possibly complete it. It probably won't look good or feel good. But hey, if you accept that you were only 'three months trained' ready, then that's cool.

You'll probably start off okay, then you'll possibly jog/walk, then you'll possibly walk/walk and eventually you might cross the finish line.

This is what I did when I tried my first marathon – though at the time I didn't contemplate walking, so as soon as I was no longer able to run, I stopped and then failed to complete.

However, if you want a solid training base then I recommend a good 6 months' lead time. Preferably longer, especially if you're starting from scratch.

YOUR CURRENT STARTING POINT

Knowing your current starting point – how fast and how far you can comfortably run today – allows you to work out where you can slot into a training plan.

For this, you need to know how long your current consistent long run is and how fast you can currently run (or run/walk or walk) 3k.

If your consistent long run is 45 to 60 minutes and you can complete between 6k to 10k in that time, then I recommend you start at the 10k to marathon section (31 weeks prior to race date).

If you can comfortably run a half-marathon then, funnily enough, I recommend you start at the half-marathon to marathon section (22 weeks prior to race date).

If you are starting from scratch, then let's get you going with my 12-week 0 to 10k training plan and build gradually.

By building gradually and taking your time, I truly hope you'll discover that 'running is for life, not just for Christmas'.

What's the importance of knowing your 3k time, I hear you ask?

This piece of information is plugged into a race time predictor which will give you your predicted marathon completion time and your marathon running pace.

Your predicted marathon pace will be the pace you'll aim to run at on your long runs.

How do you work out your marathon pace, I also hear you ask?

Okay, you've got the result of your 3k time trial, now let's go and use a race time predictor. I use the Runners World website:

http://www.runnersworld.com/tools/race-time-predictor

Complete the online form (you don't need to add the distance covered per week). It will formulate your marathon race pace from your time trial result.

As you improve, the speed at which you run train increases. This is why we have the rest and test week every 3 weeks.

Every 3 weeks, put your time trial results into the race time predictor and then note down your current marathon race pace for the following 2-week block of training runs.

Next...

How many weeks lead time do you need to train prior to your marathon?

FINDING YOUR TRAINING PLAN START PLACE AND DATE

The best way to work out your training plan start date is to work from the day of the race and build it backwards in stages.

What does that mean?

Let's work an example and reverse engineer a training timescale for the London Marathon.

The marathon is usually held on Sunday the 20 somethingth of April – as of writing this, the next one is Sunday 22 April 2018.

0 to 10k 12wk plan	10k to half 9wk plan	Half to full 12wk plan	Final prep 10wk plan	Race day
17 Jul 17	18 Sep 17	20 Nov 17	12 Feb 18	22 Apr 18
43 weeks prior	31 weeks prior	22 weeks prior	10 weeks prior	26.2 miles DONE!

You build your plan in reverse starting with the final ten-week preparation plan from your race day.

Then add a further twelve weeks of general preparation taking you from half-marathon to the full distance. That's 22 weeks prior to your race date.

Then add a further 9 weeks to get you from 10k to half-marathon distance. That's 31 weeks prior your race date.

If you're starting from zero, that's all good too.

You simply start from where you are with what you've got – a mind that believes it can and a body that will follow when you give it the time it needs. Add a further 12 weeks to get you from 0 to 10k. That's a minimum of 43 weeks prior to your race date.

I say a minimum of 43 weeks if you are starting from scratch for very good reason.

During the initial weeks, you may find you need a little longer for you and your body to get used to running. It's okay to take your time, repeat some weeks if you feel the need.

Like I said earlier, my hope is that you fall in love with running and that the slow and steady build and consolidate route is best for longevity.

WEEKLY ROUTINES

Okay, you now know your lead time and you know where you need to start on the training plan.

Next, is developing weekly routines.

The key word there is 'routine'. Or habits.

It's all about creating habits so that training for your marathon becomes second nature.

As I've mentioned, the training plan is set in 3-week blocks.

The first 2 weeks are all about pushing. Remember, I'm also into longevity too, so when I say push, I mean push you a little from where you are. I don't mean go full on mad crazy to the point that you give up because you can't move – not a good strategy.

The aim is to run train 3 days a week.

In between, you'll train to improve your core strength, you'll train movements that counter-balance all the forward running motion, you'll train to rehab weaknesses and there'll be lots of stretching to keep you in tune with your body.

Now, the ultimate purpose of this training plan is to help you become a marathon runner, so running is kind of key.

I understand that life, people, work and weather can often challenge your commitment to training.

However, if you've gone through the exercise in Chapter 1 – What your 'Success' looks like, then these life issues will rarely stop you.

Why?

Because you know your why and you understand your commitment to your why.

However, if things DO crop up, the first option is to shuffle your run sessions around so that you can still get them into your weekly schedule.

If you double up and do a run session 2 days on the trot, follow it up the next day with a stretch session only – I'd rather you miss a body strength training session than a run session.

Your second option is to shorten the run training session to squeeze something in.

As a last resort, skip the session.

Now, what if you have a marathon time goal in mind?

That's cool.

Again, find out where you are right now and what your predicted marathon time is likely to be by testing your 3km speed and using the race time predictor.

If you have a goal finishing time in mind and it's faster than your current predicted time, then you'll probably guess what I'm going to advise.

It's pretty simple really.

If you want to hit your marathon goal time, then you'll have to put in the effort in the speed, hills and lactic threshold sessions. Then also ensure you do all the endurance sessions.

It's the only way – no shortcuts.

If achieving a certain marathon time is one of your whys then I hope you wrote about it.

If you are connected to why you want to achieve your goal time, you will do all the training and not let other things take precedence.

It's that ol' neural activity feedback loop – *repeat the same thoughts often... Your brain then sends those same messages back to you as 'thoughts', 'beliefs' and 'attitudes' that you act on.*

Write your goals daily and remember to write them in the present tense...

> *'I am a marathon runner. I crossed the finish line in 3:59:30. I committed to and completed all of the training sessions that took me step by step to the finish line. I am so happy, so proud, so full of self-accomplishment etc., etc., (your words, your goals, your feelings).*

Throughout your training, your predicted marathon pace will change as you get faster and stronger.

Keeping track of your improvements is key to your training. This is why week 3 is so important. Rest, then test, then reset to push towards your goal.

Having said all of that, if your predicted race pace is wildly different to your goal race pace – for example, your current predicted time is 5 hours and you want to run a marathon in 3 hours – then perhaps you should have a re-think.

I'm not saying it can't be done, but perhaps that's a more realistic goal for a second marathon after completing at least one solid 6-month training plan.

(I really don't like using the term 'more realistic', it sounds quite negative. As I said, I'm not saying it can't be done, I'm all for setting your mind to something and then going for it. What I'm saying is that it may take a little longer to achieve that goal.)

AT A GLANCE

You should now understand the 7 essential ingredients to include in a running training plan:

- endurance
- speed
- power
- strength
- mobility
- agility
- flexibility

and why they've all been included in the plans I provide at end of this book.

Also, that everyone's starting place is different depending on your running history. You need to know your current starting position ie., your speed over 3k and the length of your current long run.

These pieces of information will help you find your starting point.

Lastly, weaknesses or body imbalances will cause injury. Let's get on top of them right from the very start.

Things for you to do before you get started:

1. Test your 3k speed.
2. Choose the training plan according to your starting point
3. Book a marathon around the date that provides you with the optimal training time you need to achieve your marathon goal.
4. Do the simple body movement assessment to test for any weaknesses or body imbalances. If there are weaknesses, then ensure you're doing the body strength workouts – they target these areas. Practice what you need to improve.

WHAT'S NEXT

The training plan is available in Chapter 6. The plan, but before you run off (see what I did there), I'd like to delve a little further into how to improve your running with technique.

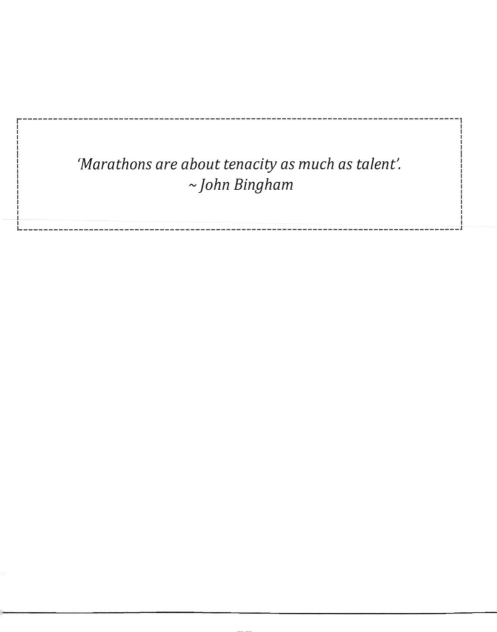

'*Marathons are about tenacity as much as talent*'.
~ *John Bingham*

CHAPTER 3. THE TECHNIQUE

IMPROVE YOUR RUNNING PATTERN TO GET FASTER,
STRONGER AND REDUCE INJURIES

The quote by John Bingham is true. You will have to dig deep and be tenacious to run and finish a marathon.

However, you can stack the odds in your favour by being totally committed to your training plans and improving your technique.

If you're constantly getting injured from running then it will either be due to imbalances of weaker/stronger muscles and/or your technique needs tweaking.

Like most, I imagine you began running by going out for a little jog about.

From there you may have learnt how to do some varied speed work to help you go quicker.

However, there is an optimal running pattern that you can create with your body that, when you've got it going on, will help you get faster, stronger and reduce injury risks.

First and foremost it's about posture. Get these 2 things working:

- standing posture
- running posture

Add these spicy ingredients:

- cadence
- foot landing
- arm swing

Then watch and feel your running improve.

It's always a thrill to see people 'think' about running.

Thinking about running is being open to the idea that to become a better runner it's not always about all the miles you run. It's not always about increasing speed, adding tempo runs, doing more and more...

It's actually about getting the foundations right.

The body moves beautifully, efficiently and effectively when you:

- think about posture – not necessarily about mileage
- think about core – not necessarily about glutes, quads and hamstrings
- think about arm and body position – not necessarily about running shoes

Technique is the answer!

Running is about connecting with your body's ability to feel, absorb and harness the natural power of its elasticity to create beautiful movements.

Running, done well, is a graceful art form of moving the body forward.

My love for running technique grows each and every time I see people change their running style over the course of a day.

At the start of a session, I can literally hear knee joints screaming 'NO MORE' as I watch the majority of runners land a heel strike position (I explain more on this term shortly).

As the day progresses and the technique changes are implemented, I see running steps being taken with beauty, ease and elegance and I hear the knee, ankle and hip joints give a communal sigh of relief.

So, let's get into this.

POSTURE

STANDING POSTURE

This is going to be a little bit interactive – it may help to have a friend or partner around.

You'll need:

- a drop line (which you can build using a length of string and a weight)
- a camera to photograph the results

We're going to determine your natural posture.

Build a drop line and set it up

1. Grab a length of string (the length of a door opening drop) and tie a weight on the end.
2. Attach the drop line to the door frame (using a nail or a drawing pin) ensuring the line is in the middle of the opening. (I'm actually using a weighted tape measure in the photo – that works too.)
3. Wear tight fitting clothing (lycras if you've got them), you want to see the shape of your back and all the alignment points of your body listed below.
4. Stand behind the drop line, then turn side on to it.
5. Ask your partner to get you to stand with the drop line aligned with your hip bone.
6. Stand with feet at hip-width apart.
7. Relax and take the photo.

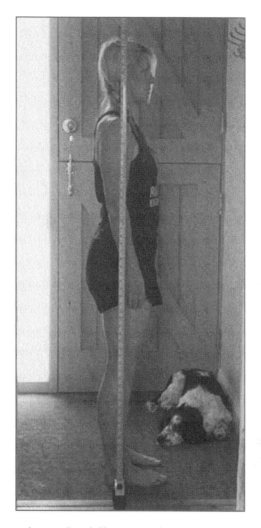

Now compare where the following alignment points are in comparison to the drop line:

- ear
- shoulder
- elbow
- hip (your drop line should line up with your hip)
- knee
- ankle

Also, have a good look at the shape of your back.

Which of the four types of postural alignment pictures best reflects the photo of your postural alignment?

The common injury traits and some recommended rehab for each type of postural alignment are listed below the picture box.

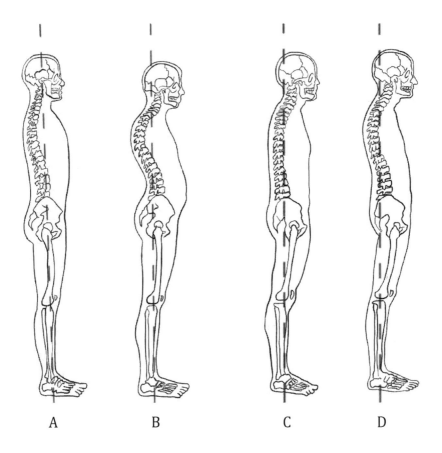

A   B   C   D

- A = Ideal alignment
- B = kyphotic-lordotic posture
- C = flat back posture
- D = sway back posture

Type A. ideal alignment

If you got this one, well done! This is a perfect posture.

Type B. kyphotic-lordotic posture

Kyphosis is shoulders rolled and head forward out of alignment with the shoulders, you look a little hunchbacked when viewed side on.

Lordosis is a deep curvature of the lower part of the spine.

Likely tight muscles of a kyphotic-lordotic posture include thigh muscles at the top of the leg, the deep hip flexors, lower back muscles, front chest muscles and back of the neck muscles.

The likely weak muscles include glutes (your butt), hamstrings (back of legs), abdominals (tummy) and upper back.

Recommendation: Regular stretching and massage to open up the chest and relax the over-stretched back, neck muscles, and hip flexor muscles. Strengthening exercises to address the weak muscles.

A great stretch for this posture is the one I call 'chicken wings'. Put your hands on your butt, fingers pointing down to the ground and either pull your elbows into the midline of your back, or have a friend or partner push your elbows together into the midline of your back. Hold for 5 seconds and release... ooooh it feels good.

Stretch	Strengthen
Hip-flexor lunge	Single-leg bridge
Downward dog	Single-leg Romanian deadlift
Chicken wings	Leg raises
Neck stretches	Prone lat pull down

Type C. flat back posture

Flat back posture, or posterior pelvic tilt, is an improper alignment of the pelvis and can lead to wear and tear of the pelvic joints.

This posture will limit your body's ability to act like a spring – you're not absorbing the shocks and spreading them across the body.

Without this spring you're likely to be overloading your joints.

The back of your leg muscles may be overworking, all leading to an increased risk of overuse injury.

Recommendation: Stretching and core strengthening exercises with the aim of reducing the strains on your ligaments and tendons. A brilliant stretch for this posture is the 'back curl on stability ball'. Lie on your back over a stability ball keeping your feet flat on the ground. The ball provides a great curve for your spine to flow over.

Stretch	Strengthen
V-sit forward lean	Side-plank taps
Back curl on stability ball	Plank
Chicken wings	Leg raise
Cobra	Prone back raise

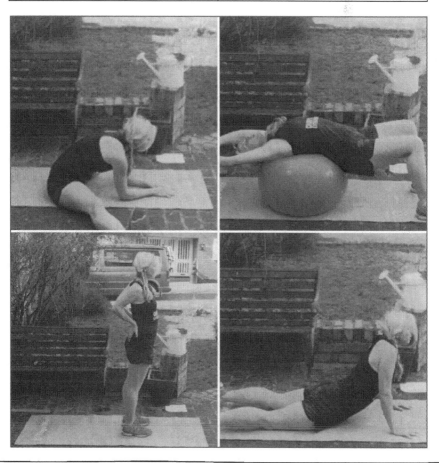

Type D. sway back posture

Sway back is when your lower back is hyperextended (exaggeratedly curved). Your poor low-back joints will be overloaded and there'll be weakness in your glutes.

You'll be at increased risk of mid-back pain because you'll be over-hunching somewhere in your mid-back. You'll probably be overworking the neck muscles too, which can lead to head and neck aches and pains.

Recommendation: Stretching and core strengthening exercises with the aim of reducing the strains on your back's ligaments and tendons.

If you have this posture, a stretch you'll get great benefit from is the 'downward dog'. Standing with your feet together, put your hands on the ground and walk the hands forward until you create an upside down V (butt high up in the air). Try to lower your heels to the ground, whilst stretching out the arms. Keep your neck in line with your spine by looking at your knees in that inverted V-position.

Stretch	Strengthen
Downward dog	Single-leg bridge
Child's pose	Side lunge
Chicken wings	C-sit
Neck stretches	Y and T arms

Stretch

Okay, now we know where you're starting from, we can work on improving any weak or tight areas during your body strength workouts and stretching.

You may have some remedial work to do but that's okay

Download
You can grab a printable PDF version of all of the above, including the strengthening exercises in the resources section at the end of this book.

It's all about understanding that your body is a continual work in progress, whether it's remedial or maintenance.

Now... let's get you into your best running posture.

RUNNING POSTURE

Let's go back to your natural standing position – like we did for the postural assessment above.

Step 1

Stand with feet a little apart. Look down and notice where your feet are pointing.

Are they straight ahead or a little turned out?

Is one more turned out than the other?

This is your natural standing position and when you run, your feet will land in the position that you naturally stand in.

Step 2

Pick up your feet one at a time and place them into a toe forward position (if needed).

The aim is to get you running with your toes pointing in the direction you want to go, so practice standing that way. It's all about creating the habits that are good for your body.

Step 3

Raise your arms in the air, feel very tall, then lower the arms back to your side.

The aim is to get your body to feel very tall when your arms are up and keep that feeling of tallness as you lower your hands back down to your side. Relax your shoulders without slumping down and losing that tallness.

Step 4

Place your fingertips on the front protruding part of your pelvis (hip bone).

This is the tilt point of your body.

Step 5

Engage your core.

Pull your tummy in towards your spine and... well... there's probably a better description for this bit, but it's the best one that I use and everyone gets... pretend that you need to stop weeing mid-wee.

Step 6

Drop your eyes and look towards your feet.

It's important not to move your body to look down. Take a look by dropping your head and eyes.

Can you see the midway point of your shoelaces – Yes or No?

If yes, then you're all good to go to Step 8.

If no, move on to Step 7.

Step 7

Tilt your body forward from your hip bone.

Using the fingertips that you placed on your hip bone (your tilt position), slowly push back and lean the body forward from your tilt point until you can see the midway point of your shoelaces.

Step 8

Lift your head up and look out to the horizon.

We're almost ready to move.

> **Step 9**
>
> *Bend your arms up to 90° beside your body.*
>
> (This will stop you face-planting when you take off.)

> **Step 10**
>
> *Fall forward leading with the chest.*
>
> The aim is to fall forward until you need to take a step.

Then... keep taking those steps in a runny-type style.

You're now running in a great running postural position. YAY! I've listed 10 steps, but honestly, they won't take you very long to do – a couple seconds of preparation before you move. Go through the quick running posture check list and you're ready to run:

- feet forward
- tall body
- engage core
- tilt from hip
- look to where you're going
- fall into running

Righto, you're now moving and looking pretty darn good with your running posture, but what usually happens during a run – especially the long runs you'll do when training for a marathon – is that your posture starts to wane.

Have this check list ready in your mind. You don't have to stop and put your body back into position. Simply go through your check list and make little tweaks to your body's position on the move.

Download

There's a downloadable 10-point check list and video available in the Resources section of this book.

DAILY POSTURE

Now I took you through these steps to set your body up to run, but I've mentioned before that the patterns we hold all day everyday impact our body.

If you find yourself standing around, go through your check list and put your body into a ready to run position.

(Perhaps without the arms held at 90°, unless you're getting ready to move – that might look just a little weird).

You'll look taller. Your chest will be more open, your shoulders will be down, back and relaxed. You'll be engaging your core, therefore supporting your lower back. It changes your look.

I've been told by my clients that they look and feel more confident in this position. I know it's how I feel too.

If you spend a lot of time sitting at a desk – go through the check list. See the difference in your body position. Feel the difference along your back as you engage your core, sit taller, open your chest, relax and pull back your shoulders.

Feels good, doesn't it?

Your hours and hours of daily patterns impact your body, possibly even more than the relatively short time that you are exercising.

Think posture! All day every day.

Okay, I'll get off my little soapbox now.

It's time to spice things up.

SPICY TECHNIQUE INGREDIENTS

CADENCE

Cadence is the number of times your feet hit the ground in a minute.

There is an optimum count at which the feet of the best long distance runners hit the ground.

That count is 180bpm (beats per minute).

I may not be the best runner, but I'm certainly going to copy the best.

There are 2 ways in which you can get a gauge of 180bpm.

First is by using a metronome – I use a metronome app downloaded to my phone.

I always carry my phone when I run. It's a safety thing for 'just in case' scenarios – just in case I get lost, just in case I hurt myself or just in case somebody important ie., kiddo, wants me to interrupt my run and be mummy taxi.

I always carry my phone in my backpack and when I'm using the metronome app I wonder what people think as I run past them with my backpack ticking away.

The second is listening to songs at 180bpm.

I'm a bit of a surfy rock chick – well I can stand on a surfboard for a little bit then face-plant fall off.

I'm also getting on in years, so my favourite 180bpm playlist probably reflects these characteristics:

- Give it Away... Red Hot Chilli Peppers
- River Deep, Mountain High... Tina Turner
- Rock and Roll... Led Zeppelin
- Love is a Battlefield... Pat Benatar
- Rock Lobster... B52's
- Breaking the Girl... Red Hot Chilli Peppers
- Foxy Lady... Jimi Hendrix

Spotify or *jog.fm* is great for place for getting a 180bpm playlist.

Personally, I don't listen to music when I run. I love the sound of nature far too much. I also often run alone, so being aware of things around me is important. Case in point...

> *Standing on the shores of the Amazon River, during my 5th marathon in 5 days. I was tired. I was in pain. I was scared out of my skin having just had an extremely close encounter with an anaconda.*
>
> *I was only half way through the 50 river crossings marked out for the day – the rivers are where the caiman live.*
>
> *There was also more thick jungle for me to run through – the jungle is where the jaguars live.*
>
> *The sounds of anything that may have thought that I could be its lunch was the only thing I wanted to hear at that stage.*

Instead of bunging in some headphones, I hum songs in my head when I need to keep my cadence on track.

FOOT LANDING

Are you a:

- heel striker – your heel hits the ground first?
- midfoot striker – your foot lands flat on the ground?
- forefoot striker – you land nearer the balls of your feet?

Do you even know?

Here's a quick little task for you to do.

1. Set your phone up on video (if you've got a 'slo-mo' recording option set it to that).

2. Prop it up somewhere where you can video a side view of yourself running past (making sure you can see your feet).
3. Watch it back and see where your foot lands.

Now, I see a lot of runners who have hip, knee, feet and iliotibial band (ITB) problems.

(The ITB runs along the outside of the leg from the pelvic bone to the lower leg bone, the tibia.)

Tight muscles, overstressed joints and poor technique are the usual suspects for these aches and pains.

Hitting the ground with the heel first and a straight leg slightly out in front of the body (heel strike) is the most common foot landing pattern I see.

When I do, I can literally hear ankle and knee joints scream out in pain.

It's like putting the brakes on with every step you are taking, not to mention the lack of spring or shock absorption in the ankle, knee and hip joints of the landing leg.

Looking at the best long-distance runners in the world – they really must be doing something right – they land each of their 180bpm foot strikes with their leg below their hips (their centre midline), their landing knee is bent and their body is leaning slightly into the direction they are going. Forward.

By practising your good running posture, mentioned above, your body will be up, slightly forward and you will start landing more mid-foot.

If you skipped over the running posture drill, go back and give it a go – I promise your ankle, knee and hip joints will love you for it.

As for forefoot striking, this works best when going up hills, and sprinting.

Personally, I try to keep sprinting to a minimum when I run long distance, running away from poopy-pants runners or growling jaguars being the exception. But I do love sprinting up hills, so I get the practice in.

ARM SWING

Arms are such an important component of running efficiently and effectively and are often the last things considered if considered at all.

They are the counter-balance to the motion of your legs.

Remember the running posture position of tall and forward lean. If the arms are not counteracting that forward falling motion... face-plant!

Relax your shoulders, bend your arm to 90° beside your body. The arms will act as a pendulum – swing them backwards and your arms will naturally move forward in an arc movement.

The aim is to keep the arms at a 90° level moving forward and backward – not side to side.

Side-to-side movement impacts the forward momentum of your running and, in most races – unless you're jumping side to side to avoid rocks, trees or snakes – forwards is the way to go.

Letting your arms drop lower than the 90° will slow the swing movement, which will have a knock-on effect on your foot cadence.

In fact, one of the best tips I was given to help me to run with a 180bpm foot cadence was to start with the arms. Get the arms to swing to the 180 beat and the legs will follow.

In summary, most runners I know have a heel strike pattern, but that's generally because they've never been shown any other way ie., how to 'think' and optimise their running posture, their cadence, their land foot position and their arm swing.

If you're open to 'thinking' and willing to implement these spicy ingredients into your running, you'll see and feel the improvement.

It may feel weird to start, but increasing the longevity of your running life, decreasing injury and gaining the added bonus of improving your running results is, in my mind, a pretty fine goal to strive for.

AT A GLANCE

Knowing your postural body type will help you work on improving any weak spots and/or ease any tight spots in your body with the aim of improving your running and lowering injury risk.

Take the postural test and you can start tailoring your body strength and stretching sessions to specifically suit your body's needs.

I've also encouraged you to 'think' about running and build in better habits. Get your body ready, go through the check list of good running posture:

- feet forward
- tall body
- engage core
- tilt from hip
- fall into running

Add the spicy ingredients of 180bpm cadence, midfoot strike and 90° arm swing and then...

WOOHOO, you're looking good kid!

WHAT'S NEXT

Now it's time to ease it off a little and get in touch with your body.

> 'There is virtue in work and there is virtue in rest.
> Use both and overlook neither'
> ~ Alan Cohen

CHAPTER 4. THE RECOVERY

Running a marathon, or running any distance for that matter is all about self-love. Self-love is understanding then giving your body what it needs to keep it going.

A well-rounded training plan will also include:

- warm up
- stretching
- rolling
- massaging
- resting

I often hear people say they haven't got time, or they don't make time to warm up, stretch, roll, massage or rest.

I get it, we all have busy lives, and the aim of these training plans is to ensure that marathon training does not totally consume your life.

By training smarter (doing all the basics), running smarter (doing all the technique), then complementing it with smart recovery and smart nourishment, then you should only be spending quality time not quantity time training and you'll spend less time feeling sore, injured and knackered.

Here's my advice on recovery.

Start before you even take your first running step. Warm up, warm up, warm up.

WARM UP

Answer me honestly, do you warm up every time you go for a run?

I've got to say, if I don't warm up (which is a rarity) then you'll see me a little further along the track doing some form of stretching.

Without it, my run just don't feel good.

That's the whole point of a warm up. It's to help your body feel good before upping the intensity and getting stuck into your session.

It's about getting the blood pumping and getting the oxygen delivered to the outer extremities – your arms, legs fingers and tootsies – warming up your muscles ready for action.

> *I recently finished a morning training session in my local woods and was heading back to the car when I saw someone doing a series of warm-up exercises.*
>
> *Those moves looked very familiar.*
>
> *The warming up runner was one of the first ladies I trained when I set up my local women's running group approximately 8 years ago.*
>
> *I caught her up and she told me she did this little routine each and every time she went out for a run.*
>
> *It was so lovely to see that I had made a positive impact on her running, that she was still 'in love' with running and that she was running injury free after all these years.*
>
> *The point of the story... DO IT!*

Honestly, a few minutes and a few key moves to get your feet, ankles, calves, quads, hamstrings, hips and arms moving, and in the process, the heart pumping and ready for action, will make a huge difference to how you feel during and after your run.

http://nikkilove.co.uk/are-you-a-warm-up-stretch-down-runner/

I'm also a big fan of using a foam roller for a warm up, but I realise a foam roller may not always be handy pre-run.

However, if you have got one handy, jump on it and give your muscles a wake-up roll that they'll love, details are further down in the Rolling section of this chapter.

STRETCHING

As a runner, you hold your body in a fairly static position during your run, and as a marathon runner, you hold it in this position for a long time.

This running position does not utilise your joint's full range of movement.

To counter this holding position, I've incorporated a big range of movement exercises such as the squat and full body extension or the lunge jump into your body strength workouts.

I also encourage you to stretch every day.

Creating daily habits – a little, often – is definitely the way to go.

A daily two-minute full body stretch is a nice way to start and end your day and gives you a chance to tune in and listen to your body.

http://nikkilove.co.uk/hey-body-how-you-doing-daily-stretch/

What do I mean by tune in and listen?

As you conscientiously go through the stretching movements, you'll notice if an area is a little tighter than usual, perhaps there's a little niggle here or there.

Most injuries occur from a gradual build up and in most cases, you simply haven't listened to the tell-tale hints your body gives out.

I also recommend taking a few minutes post-run to stretch the main muscle groups that you use when running.

The aim is to slowly but continually move into the range of flexibility for each stretch – not get into a position hold it and then move on.

The post-run flow stretch hits the calves, hamstring, quads, hip flexors, glutes, lower back and your mid-back and chest – all the muscles that are working hard when you're running.

http://nikkilove.co.uk/are-you-a-warm-up-stretch-down-runner/

Take that extra couple of minutes at the end of your run – your body will love you for it.

ROLLING

Rolling is a form of self-massage and, as a massage therapist, I'm all for massaging your body to keep it balanced, supple and flexible.

Using your bodyweight on top of a foam roller, you move over your body's muscles and fascia with the aim of releasing any tight spots, improving flexibility and encouraging blood flow.

Fascia is a band or sheet of connective tissue that surrounds and stabilises individual muscles and organs. Remember, I mentioned before about the body's natural elasticity system – that's your fascia system, so you want to look after it.

Encouraging blood flow is one of the reasons I love foam rolling as a warm up exercise as well as its beneficial use for stretching after exercise.

There's a bit of an art to using the foam roller.

Continual slow rolling motions, changing the angles of the body part and then increasing the weight load on the body part helps you hit many of the muscles.

It's a little difficult to hit all of the muscles. This is where sports massage therapy comes into its own – got to keep myself in a job somehow – but for regular body self-management, the foam roller works a treat.

Be a little cautious though, overworking problem areas can cause inflammation through aggravation of the tissue, so foam rolling is all about slow movements and increasing intensity – without overdoing it.

1. Start off slow and easy by holding as much bodyweight as you can off the roller.
2. Increase weight pressure and maintain slow movements and good posture. I'll explain more about that in just a tic.
3. Stop on spots that require a little longer to feel a release but don't overdo the hold; you don't want bruising, you want relief and release.

Maintaining good posture, meaning engaging your core whilst foam rolling, will help keep your joints in good alignment and not put pressure on your spine.

After all, the aim of rolling is to help your body not cause problems.

Be aware that foam rolling takes effort when done properly – your core will get a little workout.

When you roll on tight spots it may hurt a little bit, but trust me, being injured and unable to train hurts more.

Warm up rolling

The aim is to roll a couple of times over the muscles that you're going to use when you run – the calves, achilles, hamstrings, butt, quads, lower leg (tibialis anterior).

Combine these with your running warm up drills (above) and you're ready to go.

Post-run stretch rolling

Start as above with the warm up rolling then increase the weight load by putting one leg on top of the other – continuing to roll.

Take note of any spot that may be feeling particularly tight and at the end of the increased load roll.

Go back and add some more intensity by moving into a slow stretch on the area.

http://nikkilove.co.uk/roll-baby-roll-foam-rolling-warm-stretch-relax-body/

RESTING/SLEEPING

Resting is the time for your body to absorb all the training and pushing that you've put it through.

Your body needs this time or it will soon let you know about it – overtraining injuries!

That is why week 3 – the rest, test and consolidate week – is built into the plans and why the body strength workouts on your non-run days are short.

Sleep time is when your body sets about doing its thing – repairing and building.

It's recommended that you get 7 to 9 hours of sleep.

This allows the brain to do its brain stuff – learn, think, remember ie., the psychological recovery and for the body to do its body stuff ie., the cellular recovery.

As an athlete, and yes *you are* an athlete, you may require a little more sleep to recover from injury, intense training and competition.

The body releases growth hormones and androgens when you sleep. This is a good thing.

These little hormones are essential for muscle repair, muscle building, bone growth and the oxidation of fat.

Oooh, a little fact about the oxidation of fat for those of us (well me really) who are getting old and noticing more and more wrinkles...

The 'oxidation of fat' process creates fatty acids.

Fatty acids are necessary for your tissues and organs to work properly. They reduce total cholesterol, they help your immune system to work, and they help prevent wrinkles, keeping skin healthy, elastic and youthful looking – gotta love that YAY!

Lack of sleep can increase your levels of the stress hormone, cortisol. Cortisol is a necessary hormone, but too much of it is a bad thing.

Too much cortisol can lead to depression, fatigue, weight gain, back pain... hmmm, not really symptoms high on my agenda to have, and I certainly don't want to run with any of them.

Ever wonder why you struggle to run if you've scrimped on sleep?

Lack of sleep can also lower the body's production of glycogen which is the stuff we use as our main energy source when we exercise. The knock on effect – lack of energy.

AT A GLANCE

Taking care of your body is key to ensuring the longevity of your running life. It's all about tuning in, feeling and listening.

Take the time to stretch and roll; honestly, your body will love you for it.

Get your zzzzs and keep a younger looking face.

WHAT'S NEXT

You are what you eat, so the saying goes. I'm not so sure if you eat broccoli, you become broccoli.

However, I do know that if you feed your body with stuff packed full of all the nutrients, vitamins and minerals that it needs to do its daily stuff, then the better your body looks and feels.

Let's talk nourishment.

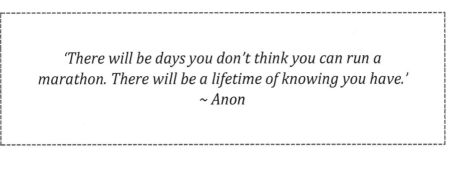

'There will be days you don't think you can run a
marathon. There will be a lifetime of knowing you have.'
~ Anon

CHAPTER 5. THE NUTRITION

FUEL YOUR BODY TO RUN LONGER AND FEEL MORE
ENERGETIC

I have a terrible sweet tooth... I run cos I cake and I chocolate. And as I mentioned at the start, I also wine and I beer.

What I've learned is how to use the 80/20 rule.

Which simply means over the spread of a week, be on point with the food you eat 80% of the time.

It provides energy, nutrients and the building blocks to keep your body strong and on the go.

For the other 20% of the time, take on board your indulgences – the chocolate, cake, pizza, whatever it is that floats your boat.

Now, I'm not going to say eat 'this' today for breakfast, eat 'this' for lunch and eat 'this' for dinner. I'm not really big on telling people to eat a specific foodstuff – after all, we all have different tastes. I know not everyone will enjoy salmon and cucumber for breakfast – me, I love it! And if you've ever endured a dinner at mine, you'll also know I'm not a very good cook, so my recipes are quick and simple.

Whack (yes, it's a technical cooking term) a piece of fish in the oven, sprinkle it with some herbs, surround it with sweet potato and veggie wedges, steam up some broccoli (I do love broccoli) and ta-daa, grubs up!

I can cook more complex meals at a push, but I need a pretty hefty push.

Notwithstanding my lack of domestic goddessnessness ('tis a word, trust me), I can share with you the principal of eating to nourish and fuel your body to keep it looking good,

feeling good, training hard and running long.

I follow a simple mantra...

'plate up protein and fresh produce'

Don't worry, I'm not going to get you to sit down, cross your legs and then chant my mantra over and over again.

However, I do want you to think about these 6 words every time you prepare a meal.

'plate up protein and fresh produce'

Below is a list of foods broken down into the categories:

- protein
- carbohydrates (carbs)
- good fats

You'll see that the carbs are further broken down into veggie carbs, fruity carbs, and starchy carbs – they are listed in columns from left to right and colour coded green/orange/red.

The aim is to stick mainly to the concept that green is 'go and great' at every meal veggie carbs, orange is 'okay and occasional' fruity carbs and red is... all right I ran out of appropriate alliterations for red (starchy carbs), but hopefully you get the gist. Eat reds more sparingly.

Obviously, the colour coding is somewhat lost in a black and white print. However, if you wish to download my good food guide PDF from the resources section, you'll see the list in all its magnificent technicolour glory.

GOOD FOOD GUIDE

Protein
Best choices
Eggs
Fish (cod, haddock, salmon, tuna)
Shellfish (scallops, prawns, clams, mussels, crab, lobster)
Chicken
Turkey
Game
Cottage cheese
Soya beans/milk
Tofu
Quinoa
Deli counter meats (slices of chicken, turkey etc.)
Acceptable choices
Beef
Pork
Lamb
Deli counter meats (slices of ham, roast beef etc.)
Low-fat milk
Greek yoghurt
Nuts
Nut butters
Seeds
Beans (kidney, black etc.)
Protein shakes and bars

Veggie carbs	Fruity carbs	Starchy carbs
Best choices	**Best choices**	**Best choices**
Alfalfa	Apple	Beans(kidney/black)
Asparagus	Blackberries	Corn
Aubergine	Blueberries	Couscous
Beetroot	Cranberries	Lentils
Broccoli	Pear	Peas(black-
Brussel sprouts	Raspberries	eyed/chick)
Cabbage	Strawberries	Parsnips
Carrot	**Acceptable**	Pumpkin
Cauliflower	Apricot	Quinoa
Celery	Banana	Whole grains
Courgette	Cantaloupe	Rice(brown/wild)
Cucumber	Cherries	Sweet potato
Eggplant	Fig	**Acceptable**
Fennel	Grapefruit	Barley
Garlic	Grapes	Cereals (>4% fibre)
Green beans	Honeydew	Oats
Green peas	Kiwi	Popcorn
Kale	Lemon	Pumpernickel
Leek	Lime	Rice cakes
Lettuce	Mango	Rye
Mange tout	Nectarine	Spelt bread
Mixed leaves	Orange	Gluten-free bread
Mushroom	Peach	Gluten-free pasta
Onion	Pineapple	
Peppers	Plum	
Radish	Pomegranate	
Spinach	Raisins	
Sprouts	Watermelon	
Sugar snap peas		
Tomato		
Turnip		

Good fats

Best choices

Avocado
Olives
Oils (coconut oil, extra virgin olive oil, flaxseed oil, fish oils)
Seeds (chia, sunflower, pumpkin, flaxseed, linseed)
Nuts (almonds, brazil nuts, hazelnuts, pecans, walnuts)
Nut butters (peanut, almond)
Fatty fish (anchovies, salmon, mackerel, sardines, tuna)

Acceptable choice

Lean meats* (beef, chicken dark meat, turkey dark meat, duck, lamb, pork)

* ensure you cut away any visible white fat from your meat

HOW TO PUT A MEAL TOGETHER

It's very straightforward. Choose a protein, add carbs (going from green to orange to red) and add healthy fats.

Honestly, this is how simple it is to put a nutritious meal together for breakfast, lunch, dinner and snacks.

Choose your protein, choose your fresh produce, whole grains and pulses, add some good fats and... Ta-daa!

A meal that is simple and delicious and provides your body with the necessary nutrients and energy to keep your body looking good, feeling good and training good.

HOW OFTEN YOU SHOULD EAT

I follow a simple pattern:

- breakfast
- snack
- lunch
- snack
- dinner
- snack

I have a very physical job. Add to that my training schedule, and I find that eating throughout the day helps keep my energy levels up and the craving for chocolate down.

It doesn't mean I forego the chocolate (or cake). Like I said at the start of the chapter, I have a sweet tooth and love the stuff, but by eating throughout the day, I don't craaaaaaave the stuff – 80/20 rule!

HOW MUCH YOU SHOULD EAT

Well, we all need different amounts. Everyone is different which is why I'm not going to provide you with a specific meal plan.

What works for me – my gender, height, weight, age and daily calorie burn will not necessarily work for a 40-year-old, 6-foot bloke who has a desk job.

Knowing your body's calorie requirements and how to optimally break it into the ratios of protein, carbs and fats (macros) that it needs, is good to know.

I'm not a nutritionist, but I am qualified to give nutrition advice which is basically cut out the crap most of the time and exchange it for better choices.

The simplest way I've found to help people is to show them how to use www.myfitnesspal.com or something similar.

It certainly beats doing things manually – looking up calories from a calorie counter book and then working out percentages of proteins, carbs and fats.

I've done this and it's time-consuming. So, I recommend you save your time for running and use a website that does the basics for you.

It's simple to use. Complete all your details – height, weight, age, gender, goal weight (if you are trying to lose some body fat or gain some weight), and make sure you record your daily exercise.

Set the ratios of protein/carbs/fats (macros) to 40%/30%/30% and it will provide your daily recommended calorie intake per macro ratio (in grams). Below is an example of what I would eat:

Breakfast	Cals	Carbs	Fat	Protein
Walnuts - 0.25 cup	200	4	20	5
Cacao nibs - 14 g	76	5	6	2
Rolled oats - 1 cup	300	54	6	10
Chia seed - 1 tbsp	60	5	3	3
Blueberries, raw - 1 cup	83	21	0	1
Coffee - 1 cup	20	0	0	5
Total	739	89	35	26
Lunch	**Cals**	**Carbs**	**Fat**	**Protein**
Avocado - 0.25 cup	59	3	5	1
Tesco - Baby Leaf Salad - 100 g	23	3	1	2
French's Original Dijon - 1 tsp	10	1	0	0
Courgette, fresh – 50 g	9	1	0	1
Carrots, raw - 0.5 cup	26	6	0	1

	Cals	Carbs	Fat	Protein
Cucumber - 0.25 cup	4	1	0	0
Salmon, poached - 4 oz	133	0	4	23
	264	15	10	28
Dinner	**Cals**	**Carbs**	**Fat**	**Protein**
Carrot roasted - 0.5 cup	25	6	2	1
Newman's Own BBQ Sauce - 25 g	42	10	0	0
Roast aubergine,	18	3	0	1
Chicken breast, baked - 100 g	162	1	2	35
Sweet potatoes - 100g	114	27	0	2
Broccoli, steamed - 1 cup	60	12	1	6
	421	59	5	45
Snacks	**Cals**	**Carbs**	**Fat**	**Protein**
Tesco dark chocolate, 2 squares	110	7	8	2
Apples - 1 medium	80	22	0	0
Tahini - 1 tbsp	89	3	8	3
	279	32	16	5
Totals	1,703	195	66	104
Your daily goal	1,946	244	65	97
Remaining	243	49	-1	-7

Exercise
You've earned 566 extra calories from exercise today.

Water consumption
Today's water total = 8 cups.

Play around with it. If you're like me, you'll have a 'go to' assortment of meals that you tend to repeat on a weekly basis. Once I know the meal fits into my daily/weekly allowance and I'm happy with my current body composition, my eating routine stays pretty much the same and on point with my training plans.

There have been many times in my life when I've got this whole eating thing wrong.

Getting it wrong helped me learn more about eating to help get my body to look the way I wanted and most importantly to do what I ask it to do.

During my 7 marathons in 7 days adventure, I really took the whole 'runners carbo-load' concept to heart.

I was super-fit but also really quite flabby.

During the 7 days, I also noticed that the more quick sugar fixes I ate for 'energy' the more my brain struggled.

At one point I even struggled to string a sentence together.

I was pushing my body to an extreme, I was not eating enough calories and the calories I did eat were not helping to stop my body from breaking down. They certainly did not help it repair.

By concentrating on carbo-loading I was pretty much on a blood-sugar roller coaster.

Taking in 'carbs only' causes your blood sugar levels to shoot up and then come crashing back down, leaving you feeling tired, weak and hungry.

I learnt the hard way so that you don't have to.

I now concentrate on plating up protein, good fats (especially for ultra-endurance), fresh produce and whole grains/pulses (carbs).

THE IMPORTANCE OF PROTEIN

I want to stress the importance of proteins for your body, especially for long distance. However, also I want to keep it simple, easy and relevant. After all, you're here to run a marathon, not receive a food lecture.

All the protein you eat is broken down into amino acids and then reformed into proteins that make up 20% of your cells.

These are the building blocks of your body. Your muscles require protein to stay healthy and strong. Your organs require protein to maintain and repair themselves.

The body requires 20 different amino acids, 8 of which are known as essential amino acids because the body cannot make these. These 8 come from the food you consume, so you need a constant supply to maintain your body's daily regeneration routines ie., for muscle and organ repair, regeneration and development.

How much protein should you have? Recent studies show you need around 1.3g of protein per kg of bodyweight, per day.

For a woman who weighs 60kg, that means 78g of protein.

If she is an active person – remember we are training for a marathon – add another 0.5g per kg of bodyweight. That means she should be consuming 108g of protein.

Food stuff	Protein total
2 eggs	12g
80g soybean	26g
120g Greek yoghurt	5g
250ml milk	8g
½ tin of tuna	20g
100g chicken breast	30g
Total	101g

Example allowance

As you can see, eating protein at every meal is essential for you to meet your optimum daily requirements.

I haven't touched on water. Let's do that now.

WATER – YOU NEED IT

Want to give your body every opportunity to stay healthy?

Then keep your body hydrated!

Approximately 60% of your body is water – the brain and heart are approximately 73%, the lungs are about 83%, muscles 79% and even your bones are watery.

Now, I don't know about you, but I tend to like all those things working well for me when I run and, you know, doing life stuff.

Drinking plenty of water is essential for your health and, in fact, for your very survival.

You can live much longer without food than you can without water. It plays an essential part in all of our body's functions and processes, including digestion and elimination.

As a general rule, it's recommended that you drink eight 8-ounce glasses of water per day, which roughly equates to 2 litres.

However, your fluid needs are affected by your physical activity (more exertion means you need more water), your body composition, and the climate.

Don't wait until you feel thirsty to start sipping – that's generally a sign that dehydration has already started to occur.

Aim to drink water regularly throughout the day.

Eeergh, you don't like plain water?

Add a squeeze of fresh lemon or lime into your glass to give it some taste.

What about cordials?

These will generally fall under the spike in blood sugar problem if you consume a lot. Too much and your blood sugar levels start the roller coaster ride that I mentioned earlier.

Sugarless cordials? Well, they have to get their sweetness from somewhere and that's a whole other can of worms to open up about the 'health' impact of certain additives.

A dentist will also steer you down the path of limited flavoured and fizzy drinks – they're bad for your teeth.

Moderation is always going to be the fallback answer.

Does coffee and tea count?

It used to be said that coffee and tea are diuretics and will dehydrate you. But the consensus of studies shows that these drinks in moderation are fine, although excessive intake of caffeine should be avoided.

Having said that, excessive caffeine can be quite subjective. The rule of thumb is 200 to 300mgs.

Personally, too much caffeine makes me anxious, shaky and it keeps me awake. Remember, I mentioned how important sleep is for body repair, regeneration and keeping me looking young, so caffeine is definitely in moderation for me.

What about sports drinks?

Ah, let's have a chat about these in training and post-training eating.

TRAINING AND POST-TRAINING SUSTENANCE

We've discussed that you've got approximately 2 hours of hard exertion energy stored inside your body and for the vast majority of us, our marathon times are going to be considerably longer, so you'll need sustenance.

If you are eating your meals similarly to me:

- breakfast
- snack
- lunch
- snack
- dinner
- snack

then a specific pre-run snack may not always be necessary, but that really does depend on what time of day you're training and when you've last eaten.

However, refuelling whilst you're training is going to be important for you to keep your energy levels up during your long runs and ultimately in your marathon race.

So, your long training runs are the best time to practice and work out what works for you.

This really is going to be what suits your body.

Personally, I carry water and snacks to eat.

Here's a list of my favourite snacks:

- bag of walnuts
- satchels of almond butter
- energy balls
- biltong or beef jerky (I use this snack more for my ultra runs)

I make my own energy balls.

I'm really not much of a cook, but these energy ball recipes are simple enough even for me.

Almond and pecan balls

1 cup pitted Medjool dates, quartered
½ cup raw almonds
½ cup raw pecans
½ cup cacao nibs
1 tablespoon vanilla extract

Method

1. With a food processor, mix together the nuts and the dates until a sticky dough has formed.

2. Add the vanilla extract.

3. Add the nibs by hand.

4. Roll mixture into balls and refrigerate until firm, about 5-10 minutes.

Almond and peanut butter balls

¾ cup raw almonds
1 tablespoon raw cocoa powder
1 cup pitted Medjool dates
2 tablespoon natural peanut butter

Method

1. With a food processor, mix together the nuts and the dates until a sticky dough has formed.

2. Add the cocoa powder and peanut butter.

3. Roll mixture into balls and refrigerate until firm, about 5-10 minutes.

I occasionally use sports drinks. I use a powder mix that has a 4:1 carb/protein combination.

I could endorse a particular brand that works for me and it might not work well with you and your tummy, so I'll skip that.

I suggest that you try a few until you find one that tastes nice, sits well in your tummy and gives you the energy to keep running.

Any which way you go –water or a sports drink – you'll need to drink fluids during your training runs so that you don't get dehydrated.

Let's have a quick look at how to carry your fluids and any snacks that you're going to use.

You can use a hydration backpack – a backpack that has a bladder inside that you fill with water (or sports drink).

The bladder has a flexible straw that you keep in a handy position on the straps of the backpack so that you can suck on it to access the fluid on the go.

Hydration belts go around your waist and have slots to insert your water bottles, and usually a little zip pouch to put food or your phone.

It means you have to take the bottle out and put it back in as you're running. It's a little more fiddly, but you'll have plenty of time to practice on your long training runs if this is what you choose.

You can carry a bottle in your hands, but I find that carrying bottles throws your arm swing off and tires your hand. Remember 26.2 miles is a long way.

I use a backpack with water bottle holders on the straps and drinking straws in the water bottles – this gives me easy access to the water as I'm running along.

How much should you drink?

Again, this is a very subjective question. How much do you sweat? What is the weather like? How long have you been out running?

The best tip I can give you regarding fluid intake is drink before you get thirsty.

Little sips along the way.

You don't want to overdo it and have to take constant pee breaks during your race, nor do you want to underdo it and have to slow down, or even stop due to dehydration.

Practice, practice, practice during your training runs.

AT A GLANCE

The amount of calories you need to consume for your body to work optimally is different for everybody.

It is determined by so many factors – your gender, height, weight, daily activity, etc.

Rather than give you a sample meal plan that works for me, I've shown you how to put a plate together and how to track your calorie and protein, carb and fat intake.

Use my mantra:

'plate up protein and fresh produce'.

Use the good food guide to build up a meal that will help your body do the exercise you're asking it to do.

Use technology to help you with the basics of giving your body the macros (proteins, fats and carbs) and the micros (vitamins and minerals) it needs.

Practice your marathon water and snack plan during your long training runs that will help keep you running strong, not running on empty.

WHAT'S NEXT

It's time to strap those trainers on and hit the outdoors.

'A marathoner is a marathoner regardless of time.
Virtually everyone who tries the marathon has put in training
over months, and it is that exercise and that commitment,
physical and mental, that gives meaning to the medal,
not just the day's effort, be it fast or slow.
It's all in conquering the challenge.'
~ Mary R Witennberg

CHAPTER 6. THE PLAN

Right, to get to a marathon you have to hit all the milestones along the way. There are no shortcuts.

You will start. You will need to pass the 5k, the 10k and the half-marathon distances.

That's why I've provided training plans for all of them.

0 to 10k. Yes, it appears that I've skipped the 5k mark. You can stop at 5k if you truly want.

Hopefully, you will fall so in love with running that at 5k you will push on through to 10k.

10k to marathon. Again, you can stop at a half-marathon but c'mon, honestly, if you're in you may as well go all in hey... that's what you're here for?

WHERE DO YOU START

Okay, did you work out where you slotted into the marathon training continuum back in Chapter 2 in the Finding your training plan start place and date section?

Let's go through a brief recap.

If you are starting from scratch, start with the 0 to 10k training plan. This is a minimum of 12 weeks.

You'll then move on to the 10k to half-marathon training plan – another 9 weeks.

Then the Half-marathon to marathon preparation training plan – 12 weeks.

To the *All runs start with warm up exercise and finish with post-run stretch

Final 10 weeks preparation – funnily enough, it's 10 weeks.

That's a total of 43 weeks prior to your race date if you're starting from scratch.

Or 31 weeks if you're starting from 10k.

Or 22 weeks if you're starting from half-marathon.

0 to 10k 12wk plan	10k to half 9wk plan	Half to full 12wk plan	Final prep 10wk plan	Race day
(Insert date)	(Insert date)	(Insert date)	(Insert date)	(Insert date)
43 weeks prior	31 weeks prior	22 weeks prior	10 weeks prior	26.2 miles DONE!

Wherever your starting point is, it's a big commitment, but you know your WHY and with that knowledge and self-belief set firm, I know you can do it.

Download

The training plans and user guide is available as a PDF to download in the resources section. Print off, keep handy and mark off as you hit your weekly targets.

PRACTICE RACE DAY TACTICS

Your training sessions are all about getting you marathon ready, so practice what you'll do in your marathon race during your long runs.

If you're going to carry a hydration backpack or a belt to carry snacks, drinks, phone, stuff 'n' things, then get practising with it.

Practice drinking – take regular sips. Practice eating – have a time plan of what and when you're going to consume. Practice running posture checks – prompt yourself to do a mental check every 15 minutes or so after you've been running for an hour.

These things are actually easier to remember to do during a race as there are kilometre and mile markers all along the course.

Every time you hit a marker do a quick running posture check, make sure you've sipped your fluid, and take your fuel on board every 5k or so according to your practised planned schedule.

TRAINING PLAN USER GUIDE

RATES OF PERCEIVED EXERTION

This is the level at which you should be aiming to run during your training sessions.

Level 1	=	asleep	Level 6	= marathon pace
Level 2	=	standing	Level 7	= 10k pace
Level 3	=	walking	Level 8	= 5k pace
Level 4	=	fast walk/easy jog	Level 9	= 1k pace
Level 5	=	jog/easy run	Level 10	= all out!

WARM UP

Using a clear space approximately 10 metres in length, complete 2 lengths of each of these exercises.

Heel walk	Toe walk
Heel/toe walk	Crossovers
Butt kicks	High knees
High knee skip	Leg swings
Walking hamstring stretches	Arm swings

POST-RUN STRETCH

Take a couple of minutes to stretch out the main muscles you use when running.

Quads	Hamstrings
Hip flexors	Calves (bent, straight)
Adductors	Waist
Upper back	Lower back
Chest	Shoulders

TERMINOLOGY

In the training plans, I use a lot of abbreviations. Here's the list and what they mean.

L1-10	Rates of perceived exertion you aim to run at
WU	Warm up
TT	Time trial
½MP	Half-marathon pace
MP	Marathon pace
Mins	Minutes
M	Metres
K	Kilometres
Mi	Miles
Build	Starting first 5 to 10 strides easy, accelerating up to full speed by the end of the distance

INTERVAL/TEMPO/HILL RUNS

You'll notice the 'interval/tempo/hill' work periods is only a part of the total running time.

For example, interval A is 40 to 60 minutes including 4 x (3 mins fast/2 mins recovery). That's 20 minutes in a 40 to 60-minute session.

I suggest that you do your warm-up drills, then ease into your run.

Do the 'work period' 10 minutes into the session.

Finish with easy pace run, then record your distance.

INTERVAL RUNS

Interval A

40 to 60 minutes including 4 x (3 mins fast @ L8/2 mins recovery). The aim of the 20 mins 'work' phase is to maintain the fast pace and strive to run further in the recovery.

Interval B

45 to 60 minutes including 8 x 400m @ L8/200m @ L5-6.

Interval C

60 to 75 minutes including 8 x (1k @ MP/200m recovery @ L5).

Interval D

60 to 75 minutes including 8 x (1k @ MP/200m recovery @ L5).

Interval E

60 to 75 minutes including 5 x (1k @ MP/1k recovery @ L5).

Interval F

45 minutes including 6 x (200m @ L9/200m recovery @ L5).

TEMPO RUNS

Tempo A

45 minutes including 30 mins running at a pace of (5k race pace + 40 seconds) per kilometre @ L8.

Tempo B

45 minutes including 30 mins running at a pace of (10k race pace + 20 seconds) per kilometre @ L8.

Tempo C

50 minutes including 35 mins running at a pace of (5k race pace + 40 seconds) per kilometre @ L8.

Tempo D

50 minutes including 35 mins running at a pace of (10k race pace + 20 seconds) per kilometre @ L8.

HILL RUNS

Hill A

Find a gentle gradient hill at least 400m in length

30-60 minutes including 20 minutes of 400/300/200/100 hill repeats @ L8 on the up, recovery on the down.

Run up 400m at L8 and recover back to 300m point.

Repeat 300m up and recover back to 200m.

Repeat 200m up and recover back to 100m.

Repeat 100m up and recover back to 400m.

Repeat the 400/300/200/100 loop. The aim is to maintain the times up and improve the time needed to recover down. Record the distance.

> **Hill B**
>
> **Find a hard gradient hill more than 60 seconds to sprint up**
>
> 30-60 minutes including 10 x (30secs @ L9 up/1m 30secs recovery down).
>
> Mark your start place and sprint up for 30 secs, mark that spot and recover down to start position.
>
> The aim is to continue to hit initial sprint distance up for each repeat in the session and improve the distance of the spot each week.
>
> Recover back to the start position either using all of the time or resting at the bottom, but use the full 1:30 for recovery time allocated. Record the distance.

WORKOUTS

Use the timings of 45 seconds effort and 15 seconds rest for the sequences described below. Complete each of these grouped exercises in a circuit x 3 rounds.

The aim is to do the same number of repetitions of the exercise in each round (consistency).

The next time you do the workout, aim to get at least one more repetition into the timeframe (improvement).

I use the Gymboss app on my smartphone to set my timer so I don't have to continually watch the clock.

I'm a bit like Pavlov's dog – the app beeps, I start, the app beeps, I stop and move on to the next exercise. (I'm also house-trained and very friendly.)

There is a link to the app in the Resources section of this book.

I've also provided a click-through link to a short YouTube video clip for each of the workouts.

These workouts are all included in the PDF download of the training plans and user guide in the Resources section. Print off, keep handy and mark off as you hit your weekly targets.

WORKOUT A

Side lunge

Single-leg push up

Lunge jump

Navel gazer

[▶] https://youtu.be/jhydfJTEEwg

WORKOUT B

Single-leg deadlift

Burpee push up

Square jump

Elbows hands

https://youtu.be/y1tcHuDma5g

WORKOUT C

Single-leg squat

Bear crawl forward/back

Single-leg tuck jump

Single-leg butt tap

 https://youtu.be/gc67ri4QDpI

WORKOUT D

Skater jump

Lay down

High knee running

Single-leg side plank tap

 https://youtu.be/LGxGD-nHf3A

CORE A

Y and T back strengthening

Side plank reach

Knee to elbow holds

Alt toe tap through

 https://youtu.be/MjYoAfoEwG8

CORE B

Laying lat pull downs

Half get up

Alt C-sit side taps

Knee V-pull ins

 https://youtu.be/U1AfQ93XZQY

CORE C

Back raise

Cross knee pull ins

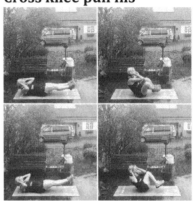

Alt single-leg V-sit ups

Elbows hands

 https://youtu.be/ZHxzHNEEOWI

CORE D

Snow angel

Alt butt tap

Single-leg side plank tap

Alt knee/straight V-sit up

 https://youtu.be/KXFIZCsVQA4

My first completed marathon – London 2002 Official Finish Time 4:59:38

If I could bottle the feeling, the atmosphere, the noise, the smell, the sweat, the pride, the joy, the feeling of absolute SELF of crossing the finish line of a race that has pushed you, that you've given everything too, that has hurt, has challenged, has taken you to your physical boundaries, then pushed you beyond and proven that YOU CAN chase extraordinary …

THAT would be the best perfume I could ever make.

It's THAT experience I want to share with you.

It's THAT buzz that I want to help you achieve.

'Don't downgrade your dream to match your reality.
Upgrade your conviction to match your destiny.'
~ Anon

0 TO 10K

Wk	MON	TUE*	WED
1	Stretch	10 x run/walk 1:00/1:00	Workout A
2	Stretch	4 x run/walk 3:00/3:00	Workout A
3	Stretch	3 x run/walk 7:00/2:00	Workout A
4	Stretch	3 x run/walk 8:00/2:00	Workout B
5	Stretch	3 x run/walk 9:00/1:00	Workout B
6	Stretch	2 x run/walk 15:00/1:00	Workout B
7	Walk 20 mins	3 x run/walk 9:00/2:00	Workout C
8	Walk 20 mins	2 x run/walk 15:00/1:00 + 10 mins run	Workout C
9	Walk 20 mins	TT 3k run Time:	Workout C
10	Walk 20 mins	1 x run/walk 20:00/2:00 + 20 mins run	Workout D
11	Walk 20 mins	Run 45 mins Distance:	Workout D
12	Core D	TT 3k Time:	Rest

*All runs start with warm up exercise and finish with post-run stretch.

0 TO 10K

Wk	THU*	FRI	SAT/SUN
1	5 x run/walk 2:00/4:00	Core A	5 x run/walk 2:00/4:00
2	4 x run/walk 3:00/3:00	Core A	3 x run/walk 5:00/3:00
3	3 x run/walk 8:00/2:00	Core A	3 x run/walk 8:00/2:00
4	2 x run/walk 10:00/2:00 + 5 mins run	Core B	3 x run/walk 8:00/2:00
5	2 x run/walk 12:00/2:00 + 5 mins run	Core B	3 x run/walk 8:00/2:00
6	3 x run/walk 8:00/2:00	Core B	TT 5k run Time:
7	3 x run/walk 8:00/2:00	Core C	Run 25 mins Distance:
8	2 x run/walk 15:00/1:00	Core C	Run 30 mins Distance:
9	TT 1k run Time:	Core C	Run 30 mins Distance:
10	Run 25 mins Distance:	Core D	Run 50 mins Distance:
11	Run 25 mins Distance:	Core D	Run 50 mins Distance:
12	Easy 20 mins run	Rest	TT 10k run Time:

*All runs start with warm up exercise and finish with post-run stretch

10K TO HALF-MARATHON

WK	MON	TUE *	WED
1	Workout A 30 mins walk	45mins Interval A	Workout A
2	Workout A 30 mins walk	45 mins Hill A	Workout A
3	Core A	TT 5k run Time:	Core A
4	Workout B 30 mins walk	50mins Interval A	Workout B
5	Workout B 30 mins walk	50 mins Hill A	Workout B
6	Core B	TT 5k run Time:	Core B
7	Workout C 30 mins walk	55 mins Interval A	Workout C
8	Workout C 30 mins walk	55 mins Hill A	Workout C
9	Core C	45 mins ½MP	Core C

*All runs start with warm up exercise and finish with post-run stretch

10K TO HALF-MARATHON

WK	THU *	FRI	SAT/SUN *
1	45 mins Interval B	Core A	1hr @ ½MP Distance:
2	30 mins Hill B	Core A	1:15hr @ ½MP Distance:
3	TT 3k run Time:	Easy	1hr @ ½MP Distance:
4	50 mins Interval B	Core B	1:15hr @ ½MP Distance:
5	40 mins Hill B	Core B	1:30hr @ ½MP Distance:
6	TT 3k run Time:	Easy	1hr @ ½MP Distance:
7	55 mins Interval B	Core C	1:45hr @ ½MP Distance:
8	50 mins Hill B	Core C	2hr @ ½MP Distance:
9	Easy	Easy	Half-marathon Time:

*All runs must start warm up exercise and finish with post-run stretch

HALF-MARATHON TO MARATHON

Wk	MON	TUE*	WED
1	Workout A 30min walk	55 mins Interval A	Workout A
2	Workout A 30min walk	55 mins Hill A	Workout A
3	Core A	TT 5k run Time:	Core A
4	Workout B 30min walk	60 mins Interval A	Workout B
5	Workout B 30min walk	60 mins Hill A	Workout B
6	Core B	TT 5k run Time:	Core B
7	Workout C 30min Walk	60 mins Interval A	Workout C
8	Workout C 30min walk	60 mins Hill A	Workout C
9	Core C	TT 5k run Time:	Core C
10	Workout D 30min walk	60 mins Tempo A	Workout D
11	Workout D 30min walk	60 mins Tempo A	Workout D
12	Core D	TT 3k run Time:	Core D

*All runs start with warm up exercise and finish with post-run stretch

HALF-MARATHON TO MARATHON

Wk	THU*	FRI	SAT*	SUN*
1	55 mins Interval B	Core A	45 mins Tempo A	17k @ MP Time:
2	50 mins Hill B	Core A	45 mins Tempo B	19k @ MP Time:
3	TT 3k run Time:	Stretch	Rest	15k @ MP Time:
4	60 mins Interval B	Core B	45 mins Tempo A	21k @ MP Time:
5	50 mins Hill B	Core B	45 mins Tempo B	23k @ MP Time:
6	TT 3k run Time:	Stretch	Rest	17k @ MP Time:
7	60 mins Interval B	Core C	50 mins Tempo C	25k @ MP Time:
8	50 mins Hill B	Core C	50 mins Tempo D	27k @ MP Time:
9	TT 3k run Time:	Stretch	Rest	19k @ MP Time:
10	60 mins Hill A	Core D	50 mins Tempo C	29k @ MP Time:
11	60 mins Hill B	Core D	50 mins Tempo D	31k @ MP Time:
12	TT 5k run Time:	Stretch	Rest	21k @ MP Time:

*All runs start with warm up exercise and finish with post-run stretch

FINAL 10 WEEKS PREPARATION

Wk	MON	TUE*	WED
1	Workout A 30 mins walk	60 mins Interval A	Workout A
2	Workout A 30 min walk	60 mins Hill A	Workout A
3	Core A	TT 5k run Time:	Core A
4	Workout B 30 mins walk	75 mins Tempo A	Workout B
5	Workout B 30 mins walk	60 mins Interval D	Workout B
6	Core B	TT 5k run Time:	Core B
7	Workout C 30 mins walk	75 mins Tempo A	Workout C
8	Workout C 30 mins walk	75 mins Interval E	Workout C
9	Core C	TT 5k run Time:	Core C
10	Stretch	45 mins 4 x 1k L6/1k L5	Stretch

*All runs start with warm up exercise and finish with post-run stretch

FINAL 10 WEEKS PREPARATION

Wk	THU*	FRI	SAT*	SUN
1	60 mins Interval B	Core A	33k @ MP Time:	Rest
2	60 mins Hill B	Core A	33-35k @ MP Time:	Rest
3	TT 5k run Time:	Stretch	17k @ MP Time:	Rest
4	60 mins Interval C	Core B	27k @ MP Time:	Rest
5	60 mins Interval C	Core B	27k @ MP Time:	Rest
6	TT 5k run Time:	Rest	15k @ MP Time:	Rest
7	75 mins Interval	Core C	25k @ MP Time:	Rest
8	45 mins Interval	Core C	90 mins @ L5	Rest
9	TT 5k run Time:	Core C	60 mins @ L5	Rest
10	30 mins @ L5 + 6-8 x 200m Builds	Stretch	15 mins @ L5	RACE DAY

*All runs start with warm up exercise and finish with post-run stretch

POST-RECOVERY WEEKS

Wk	MON	TUE*	WED
1	Stretch	Stretch	Stretch
2	Workout D 30 mins walk	30 mins @ L5 Distance:	Workout D
3	Core D	TT 5k run Time:	Core D

Wk	THU*	FRI	SAT
1	Stretch	Stretch	45 mins @ L5
2	30 mins @ L5 Distance:	Core D	60 mins @ L5
3	3k TT Time:	Core D	90 mins @ L5

*All runs start with warm up exercise and finish with post-run stretch

After recovery week 3, revert back to week 1-3 of the half-marathon to marathon training plan and hang out on this 3-week block until you're ready to crank it up again for your next marathon.

'You have brains in your head. You have feet in your shoes. You can steer yourself in any direction you choose.'
~ Dr Seuss

CHAPTER 7: THE DAY

WHAT HAPPENS ON RACE DAY AND OTHER HINTS, TIPS AND FAQS ABOUT TRAINING FOR AND RUNNING A MARATHON

There'll be a lot of tingling jitters on race day.

No matter how experienced or inexperienced you are – the noise and the crowds will get you excited and probably a little nervous.

It's all a part of it.

It'll be a part of your story at the end of the day.

Take it all in.

Being well prepared for your day will help settle these nerves a little.

First, have a logistics plan of how you're getting to the race. Know where the start line is. How you'll get there. The time you need so you're not rushing.

This is definitely a case of do as I say, not do as I do. I'm a terrible timekeeper and have found myself racing to the start line to get there on time on more than one occasion.

In fact, the last time was when I was in Peru.

On the fifth day of the ultramarathon, and despite camping on site and being less than 100m away from the starting line, I still managed to faff about so much that I had to scooch as fast as my weary legs would take me to make the starters horn.

Perhaps I overdo the whole re-check, re-check and re-check thing, but the first and definitive check is definitely a MUST DO.

RACE DAY CHECK LIST

Start with a check list of all the kit that you will need pre-race, during the race and after the race.

Have it all ready for putting on or packed in your carry bag the night before.

Many of the big races such as the London Marathon hold an event expo the day before for runners to pick up their goody bags which usually include race numbers.

If you're running for charity and have a bib to wear, get your name printed on the front and back.

If you're running for yourself and you know the top you'll be wearing, get your name printed on the front and back.

If you can't get it printed, then use a big bold marker pen and write your name.

Any which way, get your name emblazoned on your kit, there is a very good reason...

It's truly amazing running a marathon and having complete strangers lining the streets clapping and cheering you on. With your name printed on your t-shirt, bib, race number or anywhere you can get it, people will call out your name and cheer you on personally. It is such a thrill throughout the race to hear your name being shouted and it's a genuine morale booster when it gets tough at the end.

I re-check again next morning (and again, and again – though this may just be me).

Check the weather conditions and work out what you are going to wear.

I list everything:

- underwear (top and bottom)
- socks
- shorts/leggings
- top(s) – singlet, t-shirt, long sleeve top, all three
- trainers
- headwear – hat, cap, visor, headband
- backpack/waist belt – for carrying race stuff ie., water, snacks, camera, phone
- petroleum jelly or body glide, sunscreen, band aids, nipple guards, wet wipes or loo roll
- safety pins
- fluids and snacks
- post-run clothes and footwear
- bin liner

Most of this list will make perfect sense but some may need a little explanation.

I use a bin liner to keep me warm and dry if it's raining pre-race. Simply rip a head hole in the bottom of it and stick your ol' noggin through it.

It's the height of fashion as you can see.

It'll keep you warm whilst waiting for the start. You can rip it off just before you start and throw it off to the side (if marshals are collecting rubbish) or throw it in a bin.

Safety pins are for pinning your number to your top.

Petroleum jelly or body glide is for your bits that get sweaty and start to chaff when you run, places such as your armpits, where your legs rub together or, for the guys, it's the nipple area (though I've known fellas to put band aids or nipple guards over their nips to stop them rubbing their shirts), for the ladies beneath the breasts where bras and sports tops rub.

Many of the big marathon races have first aiders out along the course who will provide you with a big dollop of petroleum jelly, but I like to carry a little plastic baggy of the stuff just in case.

Wet wipes or loo roll. Just a few sheets for 'just in case' the porta-loo you need to duck into along the way is empty.

Big races means lots of people, and lots of people means lots of portaloo use, which often results in a lack of wiping products. Be prepared!

A camera and/or a phone?

You may not want to waste your time taking photos along the way as big races usually have an army of photographers who will catch you looking great (or grimacing).

You probably also don't want to take a call mid-way round the course (sorry kiddo, mum taxi is kinda in the middle of some-thing), but as I always carry my phone when I train, I carry it when I race.

I'm also a selfie queen and I like to take a few happy snaps along the way. I've practised running and snapping for years now, so it's second nature.

Don't wear light-coloured lycra pants... refer Mr Poopy pants story.

RACE DAY MOTIVATION

Remember that exercise you did way back in Chapter 1 – What your 'Success' looks like.

Read what you wrote the night before the race.

Read what you wrote on the morning of your race.

Visualise that finish line – you've done the work.

Today it comes together.

All you need to do is take one step at a time!

When it hurts – which it will – take a breath and then take the next step.

A great tip I was given was to think only about the next marker. The course will be marked out with either mile markers or kilometre markers or both.

Each of those markers is your mini goal to achieve. Then to acknowledge with a 'well done' message to yourself. Then a 'let's get to the next marker' message to keep going.

Most of the big marathons have people lining the whole of the course.

People yell and clap and cheer you on which is why I mentioned putting your name on your top. There is nothing better than getting a personal shout-out from the crowd – and they will.

There are often lots of people offering little sweet treats like jelly beans or jelly babies along the way too. Grab a couple of sweeties, give some high fives, it all works to keep you going.

Just a quick note. Don't overdo the sweetie dipping. Eating too many could cause tummy problems if you haven't trained eating them.

OTHER RANDOM BITS OF ADVICE

Over the years I've been given hints and tips, I've learned hints and tips, and I've passed on hints and tips.

Here are the ones that will help you on your extraordinary quest.

Hint #1 – Use cold (ice) water to soak your legs

After a long training run, it's good to soak your legs in cold (ice if you can handle it) water.

I've tried sitting in bath tubs filled with cold water and ice, but getting the water to cover the legs and not your internal organs is a pretty hard task (and it's not the funnest thing I've ever experienced).

I use a deep bucket that lets me get my legs wet but not my other bits.

The purpose of the cold therapy is to constrict the blood vessels and decrease the body's metabolic activity which reduces swelling and tissue breakdown.

Micro-tears happen when you train and push your muscles and let's face it, you're gonna be pushing your muscles for a looooong time when you train long distance.

Once you remove yourself from the cold water, your body's tissue warms back up, and the blood flow returns which helps your lymphatic system remove the waste by-products of the tissue breakdown.

Hint #2 – Use Epsom salts (in hot water) to soak your body

After a cold soak, go for a hot one.

You may not be keen on having a bath after every training session, but having a regular Epsom salts bath soak does wonders... well I think it does.

Epsom salt's scientific name is magnesium sulphate.

The magnesium is absorbed through the skin and can help relieve muscle cramps, pain and inflammation.

It also binds with serotonin in the brain which will help you relax and sleep and zzzzs helps reduce wrinkles... always a positive bonus.

The sulphates help flush out toxins in your body which, as I mentioned, you create when you exercise.

All in all lots of positive benefits... so go on, have a soak.

Hint #3 – Choose the right shoes

Choosing a shoe that is good for your feet and good for the terrain is really rather important. Things to consider include:

- foot size
- arch type
- foot width
- terrain

Foot size

I was advised that your running shoe should be one size bigger than your daily-wear shoe.

I'm a size 6.5 (UK) normally, but my trainers range from a size 7.5 to 8. The reason I have 2 sizes is the make, model and the width of the shoe.

If you have the opportunity to try before you buy then do it. Go to a sports shoe shop that has a treadmill and test out the trainer before you buy.

I've mainly tried through purchase experience, which can be quite costly.

However, once I find a brand, a width and a size that fits each purpose (trail running and road running) then I tend to re-buy that size, make and model over and over and over again.

Your foot arch type

Is the arch of your foot flat, normal or high?

Again you can get this checked out at a good sports shoe shop, but it's easy to do it yourself. Before you start, have some water handy.

1. Get your shoes and socks off and let those tootsies free.
2. Wet the soles of your feet.
3. Take a walk on a surface that lets you see your footprints such as a dry footpath.
4. Take a look at the shape of your footprint.

If you see your whole foot printed, you have a flat arch.

If you see part of the print missing around the arch but there is still a wedge on the side of the footprint, you have a normal arch.

If you see most of the print missing around the arch and only a sliver of a wedge on the side of the footprint, you have a high arch.

Most shops that sell trainers will have a guide to the shoes for flat, normal and high arches.

Foot width

Do you have a wide foot across the ball of your foot?

Again, this is usually a 'try before you buy' experience.

Once you have the right size and arch type, check the feel of the shoe across the ball of the feet.

You don't want your toes to feel squashed either at the end of the trainer or the sides of the trainer.

When you run, the natural flex of the foot – which is there to absorb the forces that we put our feet through – means your foot spreads a little on each landing.

You need space in your shoe to allow for the foot to do its job of shock absorbing – which is also why your running shoe should be a size bigger.

Road shoes versus trail shoes

It's important to know where you will spend most of your time running.

If you're intending to run mainly on pavements and roads, then the road shoe is the best option for you. For most, your first marathon will be a city street marathon, so a road shoe will be all that you need.

However, if you are a little more adventurous and you spend your time running off-road, then a trail shoe that has more grip on the sole may be needed.

Just a note though, trail shoes tend to have less flex and absorption, so you really notice the hardness of tarmac and solid paths once you come off the trails.

If the majority of your run is on road and your run takes you through a few mud puddles, stick to a road shoe.

I do have road shoes but I love being a grubby mud runner, so I spend most of my time in trail shoes.

Hint #4 – Tie your shoe laces correctly

Whichever shoe you've chosen you need to do up the laces, unless you use a quick lace system.

The best way to describe tying your laces is through interpretive dance. Only joking – I won't subject you to that.

The best way to describe it is the a picture.

(I've tried to use the least muddiest pair of trainers I've got.)

Notice the last 2 holes. Create a loop and then slide the lace through. It gives your trainers a little more stability across the bridge of your foot.

Again, this was another tip given to me and I have found it very useful, especially over rough terrain.

DEALING WITH ILLNESSES OR INJURIES

Despite aiming to be as healthy and as injury free as possible during your marathon training, things happen.

Illnesses and injuries are a part of human life – but for the most part, if you address them (not ignore and hope they'll go away), you can adapt and change your training to stay on track to achieve your running goal.

COLDS AND FLUS

It's important to determine the difference between both.

A cold is generally a snotty nose, phlegmy chest, coughs, sneezes and sniffles.

A flu presents with a high temperature and an achy body.

You can generally run through a cold.

However, you'll need to sit it out if you have the flu or flu-like symptoms. You really won't have the energy to run or do much else with the flu.

Seek medical advice from your doctor if you are unwell.

COMMON INJURIES

Injuries and accidents happen.

You can be running along and a pesky tree root can jump up outta nowhere and put itself right underneath your foot and break your leg.

Well, that's my version of how I broke my leg and I'm sticking to it.

We move about and put our bodies into some awkward positions.

We trip. We fall. Things happen.

Don't try and train as normal through injuries. Seek advice and tweak your training plans.

Yes, it's possible to still train – even with a broken leg. Obviously not running, but working the upper body and the core so that when you are able to hit the road again, you're not starting completely from scratch.

Remember, running is not just about the legs, the whole body helps you run long and strong.

Injuries can often be avoided by tuning into your body. By that, I mean feeling and listening to it – by working on keeping your whole body strong and working as a team (a balanced body), and by noticing problems early and not over-training.

However, if they do pop up, please go and see an expert therapist.

If niggles and injuries are treated properly you won't have long periods of downtime from running.

Resting it out ie., not running, without dealing with the root cause will probably only sort the problem temporarily.

By seeking expert therapist advice, you can sort the immediate pain and fix the root cause that created the issue in the first place.

USING ICE AND HEAT

When you have little niggles, aches and pains, knowing how to use ice and heat may be just what you need.

Use a hot pack and a cold pack – you'll alternate between the 2 for contrast.

The hot-cold contrast opens and constricts your blood vessels creating a blood pump. This bathes your tissue with fresh oxygen and nutrients and removes the waste products that your body creates.

Ensure that you use a cloth between your skin and the heat and ice packs.

For the heat get yourself a hot water bottle or a heat bag. For the ice grab an ice pack or a bag of ice cubes or a bag of frozen peas.

1. Place the hot water bottle over the injured area for 3 minutes.
2. Immediately change over to the ice pack for 1 minute.
3. Repeat in a cycle for 20 minutes.

As I mentioned, this is for little niggles, aches and pains.

If your injury is more serious such as a sprain, tear or break, get as comfortable as you can and stop movement.

If possible, raise the injured area higher than your heart.

Get ice on the injury as soon as possible and organise to see a medical specialist pronto.

SPORTS MASSAGE AND OTHER THERAPIES

Righto, being upfront and honest... I'm a sports massage therapist, as well as a coach, as well as a runny, bouncy, jumpy thingy, so of course, I'm going to recommend these services.

Not because it's an income, but because it's what I believe in, it's what I use and I walk the walk as well as talk the talk.

If you work with me or are asking my advice, I'm going to suggest you get a sports massage at least once every 6 weeks as a minimum whilst you are training for a marathon.

I highly recommend it every 3 weeks (during your rest, test and consolidate week).

I'm definitely in the pre-hab camp rather than the re-hab camp, which means, I don't wait for issues to arise. Instead, I get regular sports massages and acupuncture (from my osteopath) as part of my training.

I know it's not common practice, but many of the injuries listed below can be helped (and possibly avoided) with a comprehensive training plan that deals with weaknesses and overtraining, that builds body strength and balance and recommends good nutrition, stretching and rest as well as the TLC of a good therapist.

Oh!

Looky here. Here's a comprehensive training plan that deals with weaknesses and overtraining, that builds body strength and body balance, and recommends good nutrition, stretching and rest as well as the TLC of a good therapist.

Anyhoooooo

Here's a list of the most common running injuries I come across and some recommendations on how to deal with them.

ACHILLES ISSUES

The achilles tendon is a group of tissues that connect the calf muscle to the heel bone.

Pain in the achilles can be caused by overuse, or from the trainers you're wearing, or from a change in the arch of your feet.

Increasing your mileage too quickly, changes in the terrain and poor technique can also impact the achilles tendon.

You'll notice a thickening and stiffening of the tendon, swelling and pain when walking or touching the tendon.

Ice immediately after your run. Then in the shower, massage the tendon by putting your thumb and forefinger on either side of the Achilles and pressing whilst moving the fingers up towards the calf. Stretch and roll the calves, achilles and arch of the foot.

If the pain continues after the above, see an expert therapist and determine what's causing the problem.

ITB SYNDROME

The iliotibial band (ITB) is the ligament that runs down the outside of the thigh from the hip to the shin and helps stabilise the knee joint.

ITB tightness or inflammation is a common overuse problem suffered by runners.

The ITB can also be aggravated by running around a track in the same direction, running on a slope for long periods of time and running with worn out shoes.

It's often confused with knee injuries. A simple self-help way of determining if the pain is coming from the ITB is to bend your knee to a 45° angle. You'll feel the pain on the outside of the knee.

Easing off the mileage and slowing down the rate of distance increases in your training plans may help, as well as changing the terrain for your runs.

Stretching and rolling the legs will also help with tightness. Inflammation may require more specific treatment.

A qualified therapist will be able to assess and provide the best plan for management and repair.

PLANTAR FASCIITIS
This 'heel pain' is due to the thickening of the plantar fascia band of tissue beneath the sole of the foot between the heel and the toe.

You'll feel it as pain at the bottom of the heel especially when you get up in the morning and take your first step or if you've been sitting for long periods and again take a first step.

Your shoes, the tightness of your calves, achilles and foot arch, a sudden increase in training, poor biomechanics of walking/running can all cause plantar fasciitis.

Stretching and rolling the calves, achilles and foot arches may be all that is required to ease the fascia.

However, if pain persists, seek the advice of a qualified therapist to assess and provide the best plan of management and repair.

RUNNERS' KNEE
Otherwise known as 'patellofemoral pain syndrome', runner's knee can be caused by many things such as biomechanical issues or training issues.

You can feel either a sharp and sudden pain or a dull ache, tenderness behind the kneecap, swelling, or the feeling that the knee will collapse when walking/running.

Runners' knee is when the kneecap, which sits in a groove on top of the thigh bone, irritates the tissue beneath it due to the kneecap not staying in its groove when the leg is moving.

It will often be described as the kneecap popping, grinding, slipping or catching.

Training issues such as weak thigh muscles, may not be providing the support needed to keep the kneecap in its groove.

Tight hamstrings, calves, and ITB may also be pulling on the leg, again leading to poor tracking of the kneecap.

These issues can be improved with remedial work.

It's why I chose the exercises that I do. Single-leg exercises will show if you have weaknesses. The regular stretches help with tightness issues.

Biomechanical problems such as the size of the kneecap, the width of your hips, the condition of your cartilage and the shape of the instep of your foot, may also cause runner's knee.

As always, a qualified therapist will be able to assess and provide the best plan of management and repair for runner's knee.

SHIN SPLINTS

Otherwise known as 'medial tibial stress syndrome' is an overuse injury and preventable.

Shin splints usually present as soreness, tenderness, redness and swelling along the inside of the shin.

It's usually brought on by increases and changes to your running habits that your body is not quite coping with such as increasing mileage and frequency of training, or changes in surface and terrain.

The most effective treatment for shin splints is RICES:

- rest
- ice
- compression
- elevation
- stretch

Ease back on the running. Ice and elevate after your session. Wear compression socks (I totally love them). Stretch and roll the whole back chain of the leg, in particular, the calf and also roll the arch of your foot.

If these methods don't ease the pain, then please seek advice from a qualified therapist, as shin splints can escalate to stress fractures which really is not the direction you want to be heading.

SPRAINS/STRAINS/BREAKS

Going over on your ankle, jumping over obstacles, changing direction quickly, slipping on slippery surfaces – these are accidents that runners often have to deal with.

If you sprain, strain or break something you'll feel a sharp pain and generally have to stop. At this point, it's important to make an assessment – can you keep going? Do you need to keep going?

In all cases, the quicker you can get rest, ice, elevation and an assessment (if severe) the better.

I put in 'do you need to keep going?' because of my own experiences. Keeping on going is not the usual repair plan recommend. However, I've sometimes found it necessary.

On the third day of my five-day ultra in the Amazon rainforest, I went over on my ankle. I knew I'd done some ligament damage, and simply hoped I hadn't broken it.

I ran/walked a further 20 miles that day, had it assessed and strapped by the head medic who reassured me it wasn't broken and left me to choose to keep going or not.

I chose to keep going and did another marathon and an ultramarathon on days 4 and 5... and then gave it the rest and recuperation it needed.

It is amazing what the body and mind can do.

TOENAILS

I've lost many a toenail and I've found that it's quite common with long-distance runners.

First thing you should check is that your shoe size is okay. You don't want your toes to be hitting the end of your trainer each and every step you take – hence the reason for getting your trainers a size bigger than your normal shoe.

Despite having found my perfect shoe size, I've still lost toenails – mainly after running ultra distances or consecutive marathons.

It is a common occurrence. Don't be overly concerned. Trust me, the toenail underneath grows back.

However, I've also noticed both from my own experience and speaking to other runners that once you lose a toenail, you'll find that you'll often lose it again, especially if you pursue long distances.

The best solution I've come up with is that on my long runs ie., marathon distance, I tape the toes that I know are prone to losing their nails.

BLISTERS

Getting the right shoe helps reduce the chance of blisters, but at some point, you'll end up with one.

If you can feel a blister forming on your run and you're carrying a plaster, stop and put it on. Otherwise, deal with it when you get home.

If it's a big blister, use a sterile pin (use alcohol to clean it) to pop the skin and use your thumb to gently press out the fluid (have a tissue handy).

Leave the skin on, cover the area with antiseptic powder or cream and leave. If you need to put shoes back on, cover the area with a plaster.

Use tape, a band aid or a compeed plaster to cover it on your next run and when you get home re-treat it with antiseptic powder or cream.

If it's a tiny blister or a blood blister, don't drain, just use the antiseptic powder or cream.

If the top layer of skin comes off, then make sure you clean the area with water and treat it with antiseptic powder or cream. You'll need to cover the open wound – a compeed plaster is best to use in this case.

If you get a blister under your toenail, best advice is to get it seen to by a professional.

In all cases, soak your feet in Epsom salts and hey, whilst you're at it, soak your whole body. The stuff is brilliant for your skin – blistered and otherwise.

STITCHES/CRAMPS

Stitches usually come about from shallow breathing.

They usually occur early in a run and are often caused by going off too fast and not getting into your breathing rhythm.

Slow it down and get your breath into a rhythm.

I would say catch your breath, but that always invokes an idea of trying to gulp for breath.

As illogical as it sounds, do the opposite. Concentrate on pushing the breath out (deep breath out). The in breath will flow in much easier.

Stitches can also occur from what, how and when you eat and drink.

It all comes back to losing your breathing rhythm.

When you're taking on fluids or food on the move, you can disrupt your breathing pattern. Again, this is why you practice what you're going to do when you run your marathon.

I've also found that if I eat certain foods too close to my scheduled run, I'll get a stitch.

Some sports drinks I've tried on runs have had a similar effect.

Practice. Take note of what affects you and how. Then practice some more.

Cramps are often a sign of dehydration which leads to muscle fatigue. Cramps will normally show up in the latter stages of a long period of exercising or at the end.

This may be due to pushing harder or further under race conditions than you have trained. This is one of the reasons you train at your race pace. Practising long runs helps you push the boundaries of your fatigue level.

Tight muscles can often lead to cramp even when you're not exercising. This can usually be alleviated with stretching or a massage.

However, there may be other causes, if you're cramping regularly during or not during exercise, such as your electrolyte levels being too low through excessive sweating or excessive water consumption.

If you are continually cramping, then it's best to seek some medical advice.

DEHYDRATION

I've seen some quite disturbing sights of people suffering from dehydration – vomiting, collapsing.

Doing the ultra-marathons that I do, I've pushed my dehydration boundaries on more than one occasion. I've struggled to think and my speech has become very laboured.

Simple solution. Drink!

In extreme heat, I use water and salt tablets, but for my usual run arounds at home, I've found water is sufficient for me.

If you are a very heavy, salty sweater when you train – your sweat leaves marks on your face or clothing (salt stains) – then you may need to add electrolytes to your water or use sports drinks.

I'll keep labouring this point. Take note of what happens to you when you train. Make adjustments and then keep practising.

The easiest way to recognise if you're hydrated or dehydrated is to take a wee peek at your wee. The general rule of thumb is that your wee should be a pale yellow colour, not a deep yellow.

If you find that your wee is dark at the end of your long runs, then you may need to consider taking on more water during your runs.

Practice, and keep practising.

A quick note to point out – you can overhydrate which is not good for you and your body. It's called hyponatremia.

Drinking too much water impacts the balance of sodium and fluid in your body causing your cells to swell. This really isn't good for the ol' noggin and can cause serious neurological problems.

Signs of over hydration can be similar to dehydration such as nausea, tiredness and irritability. It's important to note how much water you are drinking.

POST-RACE COME-DOWN
Yay!!!

So you did it. You ran your race.

This event has been pretty much in the forefront of your mind for at least the last 6 months of your life and for the first few days you'll be on top of the world.

Showing your medal.

Telling your story.

Receiving praise and cheers from those that weren't there on the day.

You'll be processing everything you've done.

And then there'll be a bit of a void.

Yes, you're doing your post-race training, but you'll start to wonder what's next?

Here's my little trick to help get me outta the post-race comedowns...

I get all excited about the next one.

If you're like me, and you've totally fallen in love with running and the 'feels' it brings you, then you'll probably want to look for your next challenge.

And, if you're like me and love to travel the world and experience new places, then there's no better way to do it than by foot.

Which leads me on rather nicely on to...

TOP 10 SUPER COOL WORLD MARATHONS

For me, running is about fitness, personal challenge and a love of adventure.

I haven't run all of the marathons I'm about to mention... yet!

However, I have run in quite a lot of the locations.

I backpacked around the world in my early 20s. I've done a fair bit of travelling since then and I intend to do a lot more in the future.

I never go anywhere without my trainers!

It's the best way I know to get up close and personal with the places I visit.

As for the list, I'm going to be a little partisan here and put my favourite marathons first. The remainder of the list is courtesy of www.livestrong.com.

1. London Marathon (April)

For a beautiful historical tour of London, this is the race. It's flat. It's noisy – crowds line the route the entire way. It was my first marathon, so it will always be top of my list.

2. Great Ocean Road Marathon (May)

Ocean views and running, 2 of my favourite things. It's a tough, hilly course, but the scenery is spectacular. Oh and it takes place in my hometown, Victoria, Australia, so I'm a bit partial.

3. Boston Marathon (April)

This marathon will require you to be 'good for age'. Yep, you have to prove yourself to get into this one which is why it's on the list. It's not a first timers' race, but it may be a bucket list goal for you now that you love running.

4. Athens Authentic Marathon (November)

I guess you really can't go past the original home of the marathon. This course follows the original 26.2 miles run by the Greek soldier Pheidippides in 490 BC – from the ancient city of Marathon to Athens.

5. Great Wall Marathon (May)

It's supposedly one of the toughest marathons in the world. There are 5,164 steps to climb along the Great Wall, ending with a run through Chinese villages. This certainly ticks my personal value of living a life of adventure.

6. Dublin Marathon (October)

Apparently, it's the flat course, scenery and the people that put this race high up the ladder. Though I've not run the marathon, I have run through the city and there is no doubting it is a pretty city. Add the opportunity of a pint of Guinness at the end and I can definitely see the appeal.

7. Rome Marathon (April)

Rome, like London, is a history lesson packed into a personal challenge. You'll take in the Coliseum, the Spanish Steps, the Trevi Fountain, the Pantheon and St Peter's Basilica. It's another location where I have run but not participated in the marathon.

8. Big Five Marathon (June)

This marathon in South Africa is named after the big 5 African game animals – the leopard, lion, rhino, elephant and buffalo. It's set in the Limpopo province's Entabeni Safari Conservancy. Supposedly, you might get 'lucky' and run alongside antelope, giraffes, zebras and lions.

I was 'lucky' to be hissed and growled at by something (I'm guessing it was a jaguar) in Peru – all I can say is remember to do your speed work so you don't get bitten on the bum.

But hey, what a rush it would be to see 'some' of these animals.

9. Puerto Rico Marathon (March)

I've added this one, because I've been to South America – loved it and want to go again. Amazing coastal scenery (which I love), heat (which I love) and the opportunity to recover sipping a pina colada. Sounds like my kinda race.

10. New York Marathon (November)

It's the largest marathon in the US, more than 50,000 other running nutters will join you as you run through the 5 boroughs of New York City. With 2 million spectators lining the streets and cheering you on, you'll never get a more joyous way to see the city!

11. Honolulu Marathon (December)

I know I said I was only going to provide a list of 10, but then I saw this one and I remembered how much I loved running around Honolulu and, well you know – coastal views, heat and running – I had to include it.

Held on Hawaii's biggest island, Oahu, you'll run along Ala Moana Beach Park, Waikiki Beach, Koko Head Crater and Diamond Head finishing at Kapiolani Park.

KEEP ON RUNNING

Your body is your tool and the more you get connected with what you are putting into it and how you are treating it, the better understanding you will have of any issues or problems it has.

Right at the very start of this book, I said that running is all about self-love. It's a comment I stick by.

You will push your body beyond extremes that most people will not understand, but that doesn't mean your body is not capable of achieving this extraordinary level.

With self-love, self-caring, self-awareness you will succeed.

Building up slowly and watching, feeling and listening to your body will help you achieve your big dream goal – to chase your extraordinary.

This is how you run your first marathon. And the ones that follow.

Run like the wind my new marathon running buddies, run like the wind.

RESOURCES

I've put a whole lotta 'stuff to do' and 'plans to follow' into this book, so I figured it would be easiest if I put them into bite-size PDFs that you can download and print off.

The downloads give you a space to write, scribble and doodle, and you can tick off your progress as you go along. You'll also get to see all of the photos and lists in all the colours of the rainbow.

You can carry the printable training plans around in your gym bag or backpack and hey, if you're caught short on a run, you can even use it for loo roll...

(and getting caught short will probably happen at some point... it's part of the training process of running long – trust me).

- what your success looks like
- DIY body movement assessment
- improve your posture
- 10-step check list for running posture
- running warm up drills
- daily stretches
- post-run flow stretch
- foam rolling
- good food guide for runners
- the complete marathon training plan
- 0-5-10k training plan
- 10k-marathon training plan
- half-marathon-marathon training plan

Download all the PDFs here:
http://nikkilove.co.uk/chasing-extraordinary/

YOUTUBE VIDEO LINKS

- Wally's story https://vimeo.com/181118448.

WEBSITES AND APP LINKS

- To help you work out what your predicted marathon race time is, head to Runners World: http://www.runnersworld.com/tools/race-time-predictor
- For 180bpm running tracks, take a look at: Spotify https://www.spotify.com/uk/download/other/ or Jog.fm https://jog.fm/
- To help plan your daily food intake to hit your required protein, fats and carb targets, head to: https://www.myfitnesspal.com/
- To set your timings on your workouts (so you too can behave like Pavlov's Dog), I suggest you purchase a Gymboss http://www.gymboss.com/ or download the app for your smartphone.
- If you fall in love with running and want to push the extreme, then head to Beyond The Ultimate's website. If you sign up for an adventure of a lifetime, tell them Nikki sent you http://beyondtheultimate.co.uk/
- I swear by the use of massage and acupuncture. Whilst I realise Leicester may not be that local for everybody, if you are in the neighbourhood and you are looking for the best therapists around then head over to http://www.townosteo.com/. Yasin Tayebjee is the man who has kept my body together, and there's a gal called Nikki Love who (when not running around the world) can sort you out a top sports massage.

- Whilst I'm a coach, I still need coaching myself – the man who helps me is Shane Benzies from Running Reborn https://runningreborncoaching.wordpress.com/
- I guess I ought to mention the little website that I've got http://www.nikkilove.co.uk/ it'll tell you where in the world I'm running next.

RECOMMENDED READING

I've drawn inspiration from these people and I'd recommend anything they've written, but it's these 3 books that I've read many times over:

- '50/50' by Dean Karnazes
- 'Just a little run around the world' by Rosie Swale Pope, MBE
- 'Fear: Our ultimate challenge' by Sir Ranulph Fiennes

For understanding and improving your brain, I'd recommend:

- 'Change your brain, Change your body' by Dr Daniel G Amen
- 'The Power of Neuroplasticity' by Shad Helmstetter, Ph.D.

For times when I've wanted help with direction and focus and I've needed a gentle a kick up the ass, I recommend:

- 'Conversations with God' by Neale Donald Walsch
- 'How to be F*cking Awesome' by Dan Meredith

For food recipes my two 'go to' books are:

- 'Go Faster Food' by Kate Percy
- '100 High Protein Breakfasts' by Louise Kang

EXERCISE DEMOS

To make it easy to view these, I've set up a YouTube playlist:
http://bit.ly/chasingextraordinary

Alt butt taps	https://youtu.be/KXFIZCsVQA4
Alt C-sit taps	https://youtu.be/U1AfQ93XZQY
Alt knee/straight v-sit up	https://youtu.be/KXFIZCsVQA4
Alt single-leg v-sit ups	https://youtu.be/ZHxzHNEEOWI
Alt toe tap through	https://youtu.be/MjYoAfoEwG8
Back raise	https://youtu.be/ZHxzHNEEOWI
Bear crawl	https://youtu.be/gc67ri4QDpI
Burpee push up	https://youtu.be/y1tcHuDma5g
Cobra	https://youtu.be/wzmGwekpT5k
Cross knee pull ins	https://youtu.be/ZHxzHNEEOWI
Elbows hands	https://youtu.be/y1tcHuDma5g
Elbows hands	https://youtu.be/ZHxzHNEEOWI
Front plank	https://youtu.be/TZ2H1MAIVUs
Half get up	https://youtu.be/U1AfQ93XZQY
High knee running	https://youtu.be/LGxGD-nHf3A
Knee to elbow holds	https://youtu.be/MjYoAfoEwG8
Knee V-pull ins	https://youtu.be/U1AfQ93XZQY
Lay down	https://youtu.be/LGxGD-nHf3A
Laying lat pull downs	https://youtu.be/U1AfQ93XZQY
Lunge jump	https://youtu.be/jhydfJTEEwg
Navel gazer	https://youtu.be/jhydfJTEEwg

Push up (half/full)	https://youtu.be/hz13hiT5lxQ
Side lunge	https://youtu.be/jhydfJTEEwg
Side plank reach	https://youtu.be/MjYoAfoEwG8
Single-leg butt tap	https://youtu.be/gc67ri4QDpI
Single-leg deadlift	https://youtu.be/y1tcHuDma5g
Single-leg lunge	https://youtu.be/poJkjalJlOI
Single-leg push up	https://youtu.be/jhydfJTEEwg
Single-leg side plank tap	https://youtu.be/LGxGD-nHf3A
Single-leg side plank taps	https://youtu.be/KXFIZCsVQA4
Single-leg squat	https://youtu.be/gc67ri4QDpI
Single-leg tuck jump	https://youtu.be/gc67ri4QDpI
Skater jump	https://youtu.be/LGxGD-nHf3A
Snow angel	https://youtu.be/KXFIZCsVQA4
Square jump	https://youtu.be/y1tcHuDma5g
Straight-leg raise	https://youtu.be/6uU9iC1UiDA
Y & T back strengthening	https://youtu.be/MjYoAfoEwG8

KEEP IN TOUCH

You've got the book. You've downloaded the training plans. You've started to get your run on and you're on your way to achieving your marathon goal.

That's great!

Here's the thing though. I'm a nosey little bugger and I'd really like to know how you're getting on.

In fact, I'd love to be an ongoing part of your team – supporting and cheering you right from the get go, and if the opportunity arises, I'd love to have a little run about with you.

Soooooooooo... **Let's get social**

Through the magic of the internet, we can get it on as running friends.

Over on my Facebook page, you can join me and other runners just like you, who are going from newbie status to experienced 'marathon extraordinaires'. You can ask any question, get support, tell your story, read other's stories, rant about the tuff stuff, brag about the good stuff and generally laugh and chat about everything else in between.

I also have this little habit of buggering off and running in some pretty awesome running spots and I'm always happy for people to tag along.

If you fancy keeping track of where I'm running (and possibly helping me when I get lost) I'd love to make friends.

- Facebook: https://www.facebook.com/nikkijlove
- Instagram: https://www.instagram.com/nikkilovefitlife/
- Website: http://nikkilove.co.uk
- Twitter:@nikkilovefit

Til we meet... happy running and love ya xxx

A GREAT BIG THANK YOU

Somehow I've managed to write a book.

Honestly, much like my first marathon, I didn't really know I had it in me.

But I've had people around me who have helped, supported, cheered and pushed me to get it to its finish line.

To my beautiful kid Riley Cliff, thank you for being you... my biggest WHY! x

My folks Vivien & Robert Love, my sis & fam Liesl, Sean, Jordan & Tahlia Warren – thank you for 'running' with my crazy ideas and loving me unconditionally.

To the awesome team who've helped get this outta my head and into the world – in particular, Colette Mason for starting me on this writing journey and for giving me the advice, support and occasional stern reminder to 'finish the f*cker'.

My wonderful friends who have run with me, laughed with me, cried with me – sometimes all on the same day – I thank you for your love and support.

To all of my clients - I've honed my skills and knowledge by working with you and for that, I am so very grateful that you invested your time and money in me.